Activation of the Sacred Seals

Activation of the Sacred Seals

by

Virginia Ellen

Illustrations by John Kudlak
Angel illustrations by Jordan Taylor

Activation of the Sacred Seals

10/02

Published by
Celestial Productions
PO Box 345
Salmon, ID 83467
E-mail: virginiaellen@celestialteachings.com
www.celestialteachings.com

Second edition published 2001

ISBN: 0-9705582-0-1

The material in this book is a guide to the Activation of the Sacred
Seals (Shakti Yoga practice), to teach mystical information and to
enable and facilitate self-healing. It is not a replacement for traditional
health care, medical diagnosis, psychotherapy or medical treatment for
injury or illness.

When practicing the postures, breathing, prayers or any other parts
of Shakti Yoga, do so with caution. Work through each step gradually
and never rush any movement. Always be aware of your physical limits
and never try to force yourself into any posture. Consult your physician
before beginning this program if you are in doubt about your condition.

Dedication

This Book Is Dedicated

To You

And Your Unfoldment

Contents

Acknowledgments

I am forever grateful to my parents for the gift of life and for giving up so much so that I could have the experiences I needed to learn what was necessary for my own evolution.

I have been so blessed by Jesus and his never ending love for me, his dedication to my unfoldment and his daily encouragement. He saw the beauty in me when I was blind to see who I really was. I thank Jesus for the teachings that I will be sharing with you. They have led me home and I now know the Divine Essence of my being.

My heart-felt thanks to John Kudlak for his valuable gift of art illustrations. And without the love, support and dedication of Rosalina Comeau, this book would never have come into form. Thank you for believing in me and in these simple and profound teachings from Jesus. I would also like to thank Cheryl (Ashtara) Concannon for her help in bringing this work to the world. Words cannot express my gratitude to John, Rosalina and Cheryl for all they have done.

The Second Coming of Christ

The New Millennium is upon us and it is the time for the Second Coming of Christ. What is the Second Coming of Christ?

First, it is the time that humanity REALIZES and EXPERIENCES their oneness with God. Jesus gave me a direct path, which lies within this book, to experience my oneness with all aspects of myself which creates union with the God within me.

Second, it is the time for humanity to birth forth the Christ Light within, which is Activating Their Sacred Seals. Within this book, you will learn how to become the vibration of God, so that the miracle of birthing your own Divine Light within your human body will occur.

Third, when the Christ Light is alive within you, then you become the Conquering Christ. You begin the process of conquering your limited concepts of self, others and life. Because the Christ Light is alive within, you have the ability to transform the energy of your fears into love. This transformation is done at the cellular level which includes the mental and emotional levels of self. You are being purified by your own Divine Light. The miracle of your own resurrection from limitation into the unlimited Mind of God occcurs in the Second Sacred Seal.

Fourth, you will then know who you are, and you will have become one with the Noble Mind of God. In this state of noble consciousness, you experience equality with others and equality between your own male and female. You have gone beyond gender. You are then Pure Love, Pure Light, Pure Wisdom and Pure Grace. The I AM will be living in your body, expressing your beauty, perfection and purity.

This is what we are called to do in this New Millennium. This is how the Christ will live again within you and me. This is possible for all of us: it is our destiny. We are all the chosen ones: we must choose ourselves. If you are ready, make the choice.

Introduction

Jesus gave me so much and I didn't realize what he was truly giving to me. It took me ten years to put it all together and come to the understanding that I have now. He gave my life back to me to live in freedom and joy. The Bread of Life (Light of God) is alive within me now and feeds me each day. I desire in my way, however small or large, to give this gift to you and to have it be available for everyone.

My path with Jesus has lead me to many changes within me. I now realize that my ego is the part of myself that needs to understand the truth of God and the truth of Self. My ego needs love and understanding to heal and change its incorrect concepts of self, God and life. I have learned compassion for myself through the truth that lies within this book. It is a way to evolve into the true Christ Self, the God Self. May you have the pleasure of experiencing your own Divine Self.

The information that is presented in this book was created to be experienced. **Jesus says: YOU MUST EXPERIENCE GOD TO KNOW GOD.** I encourage you to go beyond intellectualizing the wisdom. Go deep into your heart and soul and feel the words you are reading and speaking.

Teaching from Jesus

It is not what you know about anything that gives you wisdom, but what you know of it that gives it value.

Chapter 1

My First Meetings With Jesus

In 1988, while I was receiving a spiritual energy healing session, Jesus appeared to me. This was my first experience with energy healing. I had never even heard of Reiki or other forms of energy work. Even though I was a complete novice, somewhere within me, I felt this could help me. I desperately needed help. On the outside, I looked like I had it all together, but inside, I was filled with self doubt and fear. Zia, an energy healer from Australia, offered to give me a healing. To me, she was extremely evolved and I trusted her. As Zia worked with me, I entered a deep state of peace and moved into another dimension where all things are possible. She placed one hand on my forehead and the other between my shoulder blades as I laid on the bed. Suddenly, from nowhere, Jesus vividly appeared, illuminated by the light of God pulsating within him and all around him. His crystal clear blue eyes, filled with love and kindness, captivated me. With tender compassion, he spoke: It is time to lay down the cross.

I was speechless, stunned and overwhelmed by the power and reality of this experience. It wasn't what he said that impacted me down to my very soul, instead, it was the love that emanated from within him that touched me so deeply. But, when I told Zia what had occurred, she acted like it was nothing extraordinary. As I calmed down, I explained to myself that this must be what happens in an energy healing. When

Zia left, I set this experience aside and went on with my life. I had no particular connection with Jesus and did not pray to him and he had no special significance in my life. I was puzzled.

In the middle of the following week, I tumbled into bed and I awoke at four A.M. with a burning fever and deathly symptoms that felt like a horrendous flu. By late morning, I couldn't keep fluids in my body. I had nothing in my alimentary tract, and yet I could feel each organ beginning to drain as I would purge again and again. This continued throughout the day and by the next morning, I started to feel cold; colder than I had ever felt before in my life. Lying there weak, cold and lifeless, I was dying and I knew it. I said aloud to myself, *I'm dying.* With this realization, there was relief that the suffering and struggle of my life was finally going to be over. I began to leave my body. There was no fear, just a lightness and a sense of peace. Again and suddenly, in brilliant light, there was Jesus. He began talking with me as if he was reviewing my life and it was like we were watching a movie together. I could see myself as a child engulfed by four walls of fear. Jesus told me that during my childhood, I felt myself a complete victim with no choice and no chance of getting what I wanted or needed. He explained to me that this perception had created a very low vibration of life energy in me, one loaded with sadness and without hope. Throughout all of the spiritual and emotional work I had done up to this point in my life, I had simply expanded my walls of fear and that I was still living within their confines. Even though I had spent most of my weekends in self-help workshops and trainings, I apparently had not made any real changes in my consciousness. At this point in my life review, I was shown a box with me in the center. I would think that I was changing my life, but in reality, I was just moving from one corner of my box of fear to another. I could never get out of the box and remained confined within the walls of hopelessness and helplessness. I had yet to deal with the real issues—pain and the fear beneath it. I had always accepted what I was given and didn't know that I had the right to ask for what I needed. I had evolved as a choiceless person and had yet to address what made me feel choiceless.

Later on during this life review, I remember saying *Okay, then I can go back*. Jesus replied, **Yes, but you must change every concept that you have lived by**. I was excited by the thought that I could change, so eagerly I agreed to return. (However, I had no idea what this meant and I am still working on changing my concepts of life and self.) Instantly then, I felt myself come back to my body and found myself awake and feeling fine. Miraculously, all traces of illness had vanished.

The next morning as I meditated, Jesus again talked to me. This time, he took me on a journey into my past where I had to experience my fears. I discovered that as a little girl, I had decided I was the cause of my parents' endless pain. This decision left me feeling that I had no right to live. Once I could see my belief and feel the pain of it, Jesus would tell me I had a purpose for being here, that God wanted me here and that I had valuable work to do. He said I had chosen this difficult set of childhood experiences so I would know how it felt to be without emotional support and the nurturing that a child needs to grow. I was a victim to my circumstances. Jesus then said that I was to be a teacher and healer, and that my experiences with emotional abuse, sexual abuse, physical abuse, divorce, and the death of my three year old son, were all lessons so I would know and understand the pains of humanity. He taught me ways to heal myself and others and the spiritual principles which developed into Shakti Yoga you'll find in this book.

It was also during this meditation that I learned about the value of listening to guidance. Jesus told me that the first change I needed to make was to sell my Bed & Breakfast Business. I was working too hard, Jesus said, and then he gave me practical advice on selling my home business. Since my B&B was located near the site of Ramtha's Events in rural Washington, many people were flocking there to hear him. Jesus instructed me to advertise the B&B in a newspaper going to those attending the events. He gave me the asking price, which included all that I had originally invested in the home; the remodeling costs and the furnishings I had purchased to create an adorable country inn. His guidance was that it would sell in six months. Soon thereafter, I had an offer from a lovely woman in Beverly Hills, CA., who offered thirty-five thousand less than my asking price. I had a conference with Jesus in meditation and he said I was not to accept anything less than a fair, full price offer. I relayed this to my Realtor. To my surprise, this woman made a full price counter offer, but she wanted me to hold a second mortgage of thirty five thousand. Again Jesus advised me to refuse this offer. He said that I was not to hold a second mortgage and that a fair and just full price offer was coming. For two months I heard nothing and I thought to myself, *Well, I blew that one.* And then, there was a phone call from my Realtor with astonishing news. She said that there had been an earthquake in Southern California and that this client from Beverly Hills was offering a full price cash out for the B&B. I was amazed and I was out of Yelm, Washington in exactly six months just as Jesus had said. This was my first experience of listening to guidance and living my life accordingly.

Now that the house was sold, I needed to find another home for my son David and me. The school year had just begun and David had been elected a class officer. He was also beginning to enjoy success as a star on his baseball team and he was planning a trip to Germany with the German Club. I decided to give him a choice of returning to California or staying in Washington to finish out the school year. The move to Washington had been very hard on him and he resisted moving away from his California home and friends every step of the way.Inspite of his earlier feeling, he chose to stay and we did.

Jesus had guided me to rent a home and not to buy another one. All I could find were dark, damp, cold rental homes. Remember, I was from sunny California and I felt that I was too vulnerable to live in a dark and damp home. There was still so much darkness within me that I desperately needed light. I didn't listen and I bought a new home with sky lights, light walls, light carpeting and lots of windows. There was a feeling of warmth and safety in our new home. When tax time came, I abruptly found out why Jesus had guided me to rent a home. The laws at that time did not take into account my first, more expensive home in Washington State. I had paid much less for the second home in Washington and I ended up having to pay thirty thousand dollars capital gains taxes on the sale of my California home.

David and I only lived in the home for ten months before returning to California. I had the bright home with sky lights for this short time, but it was a costly lesson for me to learn. Since then, I listen to my guidance and usually follow it. When I don't, there is always disharmony.

Chapter 2

Steps Along My Path of Working With Jesus

As you can see, thus far each step I've taken on my path (and some of these steps have been very risky) has required a choice which leads into the unknown. Any spiritual path leads essentially into the unknown, and as you travel it, you have to be willing to listen and pay attention to what you feel. In my case, I've found that there have been extended periods of time when there is no clue to the next step. At times, I've felt unready for the next step but have had to do what was asked, that is, to make a choice. It takes real desire and strong intention to evolve spiritually. My spiritual path involved taking leaps of faith and certain costs, some of which may seem not just unreasonable, but downright impossible. Jesus assured me that, *Wherever the Father leads you, so shall He be. It is time to begin to rely on the God within, the true Source of your good.*

Approximately one year after working with Jesus, I was in my bath meditating with candles and spiritual music. In the meditation, I asked *Why do I feel so unloved? Why do I feel so separate and lonely?* Suddenly, my body began to flip uncontrollably in the bath water, my hands thrashing and splashing water all over me and the floor. Jesus merged with me and he began to answer my questions. He explained why my life had been so difficult. I was to heal myself. *Physician, heal thyself!* He then told me that you cannot teach what you have not attained. If you have not learned how to become one with yourself and God: how can you teach someone else how to become one with self and God. Again, Jesus told me that I was to be a teacher and healer. My path was one of self healing. I was to attain inner peace, understanding, compassion and love, so that I could share this with humanity.

It was during this particular communication that he announced I would channel him in the Spring, only five months away. My mind screamed: *What, me channel? This is not possible.* I was stunned, instantly fearful, crying out: *Jesus, will my life have to be like yours, full of pain and suffering?* He reassured me that this did not mean a life of suffering. My mind raced on thinking how outrageous that I would channel Jesus. After all, I was a student and a seeker. I was very unworthy. How could I become the one that would channel him. I desperately needed time to think. Then, after mulling it over for a weekend, I decided that if I didn't agree to channel, I would always wonder what I missed. Besides, I thought that if I didn't like it, I could always stop.

As you can imagine, I couldn't tell a soul. I didn't want anyone to think that I was crazy, so how could I tell people that I was talking to Jesus. It was not long afterward that a friend told me about an upcoming workshop, *OPENING TO CHANNEL.* Instantly, I enrolled. I wanted verification that these experiences were true, that I wasn't making them up and that I wasn't going crazy.

So, off I went to the channeling workshop in a picturesque, mountain setting. There were cabins nestled in the woods and a large meeting room where we gathered. The first evening, all twenty five participants sat in a circle. The workshop leader was a channel who was clairvoyant and she went from person to person around the circle describing the entity that each participant was to channel. The entities were in our energy fields and she could see them. I had not mentioned a thing about Jesus to her or anyone. As she came to me, my heart was flipping and pounding with anticipation. This was the moment of truth. This would be proof that my experiences were true. Then, she began to describe a beautiful angel that stood behind me, the largest angel that she had ever seen. The presence of this angel expanded up to the cathedral ceiling. Immediately, she saw another being walk towards me whom she described as wearing a burgundy robe as he came into view and stood on my right side. She announced that it was Jesus. I didn't know whether I was relieved or not with this news. It was just too overwhelming for me to even begin to understand what all this meant.

On the following day, I began merging with the energy of Jesus, bringing him into my body. He always entered on the right side of my body. The first time that he merged with me, I felt his light move into the right side and when it entered my heart, the light hit a huge block causing me intense pain. I felt that I was having a heart attack and the pain ran all the way down my left arm. Soon, I was assisted by others who helped move the energy blockage down my arm and out my hand. This healing was necessary so that I could open my heart chakra enough to begin to express the love of this incredible being, Jesus

On the last day of our workshop, I was taking a rest at the break. Suddenly I felt as if I had a beard and found myself stroking it with very long fingernails. Mohammed had entered my energy field, manifested in me and began to speak to me. He said that I had a large boulder in my heart chakra and he would remove it from me that day. I was left reeling from this new experience and all of the other incredible things that were occurring.

As the day wore on, I became numb. I couldn't feel anything. I was so separate from the group and I didn't feel like I belonged. Soon the workshop was over and the participants expressed their *good-byes* with hugs. I went to the man who had shared the workshop flyer on this outrageous weekend with me. He was a large, barrel-chested man. I was thanking him and as he put his arms around me, I instantly started to hysterically cry. In that moment, I felt the large boulder fall to the floor. Mohammed had kept his word. For me, this was my validation that my experiences with Jesus and other entities were real.

Even though I was beginning to accept that my experiences with Jesus were real, I was still very uncomfortable telling people that I channeled him. For months after attending the channeling workshop, I couldn't even say his name. I referred to him as the entity that I channel.

As I continued to practice channeling and merging with Jesus, he felt that I needed purification. Therefore, he put me on a strict diet: no more coffee, sugar, alcohol, cokes, white flour, or preservatives. Between merging with his light and the purification of my physical body, I experienced an extraordinary cleansing. My face broke out in bleeding sores which left scars for a time. I then began taking Chinese herbs to support the rebuilding process.

There was other guidance and instructions from Jesus to help me rely on the God within myself. I was to leave the material plane and begin to enter the spiritual plane going beyond time and space into the eternal now. I was asked to put my watch aside and told that I no longer needed it. I was to ask inside if I needed to know the time. Jesus also strongly suggested that I disengage from viewing television, from listening to music that didn't lift my soul to a higher vibration, from reading newspapers and from reading books. This was to begin to purify me of the worldliness I had lived in. As I purified, I began to experience the God within me bringing me all the information I needed. If I needed to know something about world events, either the God within me or a friend would tell me. Everything came to me as I needed it.

During my training with Jesus, I was also guided not to work because I needed to spend my full days in healing and raising my vibration in order to channel him in the Spring. (I was learning lessons in trust. I had to live on my savings since there was no money coming in and I still had children at home.) Monday through Friday, my time belonged to Jesus. He would take me on five day journeys into my darkness, feeling the depths of the sadness and pain within me. On the weekends, I would emerge so that I could spend time with my teenage son.

Miraculously, in five months, I made my channeling debut. About thirty curious seekers showed up for my opening night as a channel. I charged $5.00 admission. Never was I more frightened! My heart was pounding so hard that it felt like it was bouncing out of my body much like a slinky spring, bouncing two feet in and out, as Jesus merged with me. During this time of merging with me, he talked to me telling me to sound mystical tones to raise my vibrations so that he could become one with me. He also assured me that I didn't need to know any of the answers to the questions that the audience might have. Somehow, I was able to step aside enough to allow this to occur. I didn't remember much of what I channeled, but the audience did and they loved it. They felt his presence. Some even saw his light entering my body and a few saw his face appearing over mine. From that moment on, I had a new career. There was never a need for promotion. People just wanted it.

Within a few months after my first channeling, I was guided to move back to California. This time to the desert area. Jesus explained that it is easier to Christ yourself in the desert as the energy is conducive to the process. I have found the desert to be pristine and light where God is visibly present in the naked, natural beauty. Even though the desert was now my home, there were many in the Pacific Northwest and British Columbia who wanted to hear Jesus' wisdom through me. At that time, I was down to my last one thousand dollars, just enough to pay the rent in the three bedroom home that I found for my son David and my daughter Michelle, who had returned home to go to college. Jesus had clearly instructed me to continue raising my vibration and not to look for work, but to trust that the God within would take care of us. Therefore, I spent my days in meditation, in communication with Jesus and in writing the volumes of his wisdom. Then off I traveled to the Pacific Northwest to hold a weekend event. Jesus took me right to the edge and I jumped off. Just as he said, God was there to catch me. I then came home with the abundance I needed to provide for my family. Shortly thereafter one of my Washington participants moved to Hawaii and soon I was invited there. Hawaii participants moved to Michigan and Illinois and brought me to their healing centers and into their homes. It all just happened effortlessly. There seemed to be a plan beyond my comprehension.

Although I worked with Jesus daily for seven years and acknowledged his presence, I didn't express or feel any particular love for him for perhaps the first two years after he appeared to me. In his presence, however, there is no possibility of doubt. Occasionally I have argued with him, or disagreed with what he told me because it was difficult, but he always remains consistent and persistent in his messages. Moreover, his messages are always brief and to the point, without explanations added. It is phrased or spoken differently, arriving in language I don't use. And when it arrives, it touches something deep within.

When I began this amazing journey with Jesus, I had no idea what was in store for me. He would tell me that in the days to come, I would begin to realize the God within and be able to manifest in the moment. This seemed so outrageous, since I was living at the effect of the world around me. Something deep within me kept moving me forward, reaching for the miracle of this God that was said to be within me.

Jesus continued to teach me in my seven years of training and he is still with me even now. I feel that my life and training with Jesus is like being in a modern day mystery school with initiation after initiation. (My training like this still continues.) He told me that this is the way he was trained and it is also my path of evolution.

Very often, he gave me specific instructions on how to go about changing my life. **The greatest life-changing gift that he gave me was Shakti**

Yoga. He taught me to use mystical tones to change the physical structure of energy in my body and those around me and he suggested that I pray and sound as I did each of the specific postures that connected to different chakras. This is how Shakti Yoga was born. I began the process and as it came into form, I shared it with friends. They too had profound results.**This is the Bread of Life and it allows us to change the incorrect concepts of life, self, money, love and everything in this third dimensional world.** As we begin to change, we are changing the vibrations of our bodies. Jesus told me that healing is balancing the energy form of the body. Change the vibration of the body and the body will heal. Bring forth the correct frequency and you create the chemicals needed to master your physical body. In so doing, you master your life.

He told me that my physical body was chemically out of balance and that I could use my thoughts to create the correct flow of chemicals in the body. Jesus began to help me correct my thoughts by interrupting me when I was thinking or speaking a low vibrational thought. He would stop me and then give me the truth. The first time this happened, I was still living in Washington State. A friend and I had just seen a movie and we decided to have a bite to eat afterwards. I was feeling down, alone and without a male relationship. Suddenly, a low voice interrupted my negative mind chatter saying: *Be in the moment of now and be in the state of love. Thank God for your abundance.* It felt like someone had just shook me. Immediately, I changed my thought flow, which changed my energy to a higher vibration.

I will share a few of his many teachings which helped me tremendously. I hope they will also help you. **Jesus gave me his hand and I now extend my hand to you.**

He Delivered This Message To Me In 1989

It is time for the awakening of mankind. I speak to the Christ within you that you may know your value and your oneness, for I am within all of you. I am the light that shines within all of you. I have come to give you my hand that you may return home to the Beloved Father.

For in this oneness and this love lies all things. I shall teach and guide you and take you home to the beauty within you. In your journey home, you shall know the Christ within you. You shall know that which you are and that which you have always been.

It is time to become and express the Christ within you. It is a time of great spiritual unfoldment for all. Heaven is a state of consciousness where you are expressing your divine self through your thoughts, words and deeds.

Blessed be you who seek the love of God.
Blessed be you for I love you greatly.

In Early 1991, Jesus Delivered This Message

I speak to you to teach you of the Magic of God, to purify your body, mind, emotions and soul, so that you may step forward into the Brotherhood of God, so that you may be a Christ among men. For the Second Coming of Christ be within each of you. This is a grand and glorious communion with the light of the Father and the love of the Mother and the divine mind of God. The time has come to move forward, to know your freedom. And so it shall be. Amen

Jesus Spoke On God's Will In June, 1991.

I am with you to teach you the divinity that you are. I desire for you to know that God's will for you is love, abundance, joy, peace and perfect health. For the Father's will for you is love in all forms, abundance in all forms, joy in all forms.

Anything unlike this is not God's will for you. The Father's will for you is for you to live in the Kingdom of Heaven. When you do not allow this flow of love within all of your life, you deny yourself the Kingdom of Heaven, for then you are entangled in the beliefs and attitudes of the altered mind of ego, the small self.

Anything that is not of love is fear. Any thought or attitude that you hold in fear stops the flow of love in your life. You are then worshipping a false god, the god of limitation (fear).

To begin your journey home is to begin to notice within you the attitudes and thoughts that you have that are not of love, the thoughts that pass through your mind that are not of joy and thanksgiving. For God wills nothing but love for all of mankind. It is your limited thoughts that create a limited life filled with sorrows, illness and regrets. You can have all things in your kingdom. You are God manifesting in physical form.

Your mind was created to be in holy communion with divine thoughts of God, pure thoughts of love and creation. Begin to notice the way in which you relate to life and others.

Do you open your heart and allow the love to flow freely from you?

Or are you afraid to express who you truly are?

Do you give freely to life and allow life to love and support you?

Is your God evil or kind?

Does your God punish you?

FOR WHATEVER YOU BELIEVE, IS SO IN YOUR KINGDOM. GOD DOES NOT JUDGE YOU. IT IS ONLY YOU WHO JUDGES YOU.

When you begin to notice these thoughts of fear, love them and allow them, for they are part of you. Gently give them to the Father (God). Surrender them into the light. Surrender to the love of God and allow it to freely flow through you. Do not be frightened of the dark thoughts. Feel the feelings of these thoughts and then surrender to God's love and light. Allow this divine love to heal you. Do not hide from yourself. Love all parts of you until you are whole.

Blessed be you who seeks the love of God. Peace be with you.

Jesus Speaks On Developing The Christ Self in 1992.

As you express the Father within your being, you are developing your Radiant Body, the oneness with the Father within. As you express in your deed the Father within, you inherit eternal life, eternal youth of this embodiment.

LIFE IS THE WILL OF GOD FOR EVERYONE. DEATH IS THE WILL OF MAN THROUGH HIS THOUGHTS.

Feed your soul spiritual food of Shakti Yoga and do not seek the material world, for this shall perish and you shall be left empty and alone. The Bread of Life is within you (Manna). Let the Father within bring forth the Bread of Life to you, for your spirit feeds you and provides for you.

The Christ Self is God's highest ideal of perfect man, perfect woman. It is within all of you. The Christ Self is to be brought forth within each of you.

As you practice your Shakti Yoga and release the power of God through you, you are developing the Christ Self. You come into conscious oneness with God as you serve God. Do not live to please others. In doing so you destroy yourself. **Do not accomplish your goals to prove you are great, to brag of your greatness. Achieve your goals for the good of the goal, needing no praise, for you are in service and all your good comes from the Father within, not the material world or from others outside of you.**

To be a Christ, you must be devoted to the Father within, putting this above all others. Be dedicated and devoted to your mission and to expressing the purity of God living through you.

THE TRUTH OF GOD IS WAITING TO BE LIVED THROUGH YOU NOW

YOU MUST BE WILLING:
to change your attitudes,
to hold and concentrate on divine thoughts,
to be humble and vulnerable,
to be compassionate with yourself and others,
to trust the Father within totally,
to live for God, and
to allow God to express through you.

When you give yourself completely to God, you live in this world but not of it. You will not be involved in worldly activities, only those that the Father guides you to participate in.

When you give your life in service to the Father within, you have no life separate from the Father. You enter into the Kingdom of Heaven to share this good with others.

Blessed be you who seek the love of God.
Blessings to the Christ of your being.
Jesus of Nazareth

Chapter 3

My First Wake-Up Call

My first call to change, to expand my consciousness and awareness was when I was only in my twenties. I was living the "so-called American dream": a new home in suburbia, two children, a darling little girl and a precious baby son.

My son Warren was born a few days before Christmas and I returned home from the hospital on Christmas Eve. Upon leaving the hospital, my son was placed in a large Christmas stocking instead of a blanket. He was a Christmas present to all of us from the heavens. This was our own little angel. Joy filled our hearts and souls and we could truly sing, *Joy To The World.* It was a Christmas I will always remember.

A few days after Christmas, I was giving Warren his two A.M. feeding. In the silence of the night, my infant son spoke to me with great emotion. I heard his little voice say, *I am going to have a very hard life.* Instantly, I began to cry at his message filled with power, energy and emotion. I felt scared, sad and overwhelmed. Somewhere deep inside of me I knew this was the truth. This was my first conscious awareness of being clairaudient. However, at that time in my life, my mind (ego) couldn't be present with the pain of this message and I had not been exposed to spirituality so I had no explanation for this type of communication. I began to rationalize this experience saying to myself that it must be a hormonal imbalance. With that, I stored the experience away to be forgotten. I had no way of understanding what had occurred and I didn't share this with anyone because this was nowhere in my reference as normal. Also, I didn't want to believe that it could be true, therefore, I went into total denial.

Then, two and one half years later, my son Warren began to have unusual reactions to the light. When I would take him out into the sunlight, he began to cry. Soon, he started to wake up sick to his stomach. During these few weeks of signs, I had a dream. In this dream, I was in a hospital and Warren was dying. I woke up in panic and the fear was in every cell of my body. Instantly, I remembered the forgotten message. In that moment, I knew that it was all true: my beautiful baby boy was going to be taken from me.

Within a week of my dream, Warren was admitted to the hospital and diagnosed with a brain tumor. At first, I prayed, wept and pleaded with God not to take him. At that point in my life, I still believed God was outside of me somewhere in heaven with a long beard and a staff.

You read about these things, never believing that they will happen to you. Well, it was happening to me and I was forced to feel. I felt helpless as I watched my son deteriorate. I wanted to stop the endless hours of what to me was torture. I became extremely angry at God and the Catholic Church. There were no answers, no compassion or kindness in the priest I sought counsel with. The only answer I got was that this was God's will. Who was this God who would make a child suffer so? I had a million questions about life, God and religion. I left my church because the God that I was raised to believe in was useless to me now.

Warren's illness lasted nine months. There were six surgical procedures and numerous radiation treatments. The pain was overwhelming to me. My heart was torn apart. As I write this, there are tears in my eyes. I am still healing and embracing the truth that Warren hasn't left me and that he is with me always. I have the ability to communicate with him, so I know that this is true. Yet, some part of me is still holding on to wanting him here to hold and love in the physical form. I am just now beginning to be willing to let the pain completely dissipate.

Chapter 4

A Blessing

After my son Warren's death, my husband and I decided to adopt a child. We investigated the possibilities and they were very bleak. We went to many different adoption agencies and found that the only children available for adoption at that time were children of mixed race or with physical problems. After our traumatic experience with Warren, we felt that it would be too much to take on a child like these. We then gave up on adopting a child.

Then, on the first anniversary of baby Warren's death, God answered my prayers. A college friend of my husband's, who had adopted a baby boy through an attorney the year before called. A miracle had just occurred and they told me that their attorney had just called telling them of a baby boy that had been born that morning at UCLA Medical Center. The attorney ask if they wanted the child. Our friends weren't ready for another baby and told the attorney about us. I immediately thanked them and called my husband at work. The next day we were on our way to Beverly Hills to see the attorney. She took all of our history and then she said that she would be giving the mother five families to choose from. Neither doubt nor hope was in my mind. I just let it go to focus on handling my emotions dealing with the loss of Warren.

Since this was the weekend of the anniversary of our son's death, we planned to go away on a weekend holiday with our daughter, Michelle. We were trying to create a normal life again for both ourselves and Michelle.

We went to our favorite hide-away, a ranch style resort called Warner Springs in Southern California. At Warner Springs, there are large outdoor mineral pools. I was soaking in one of the pools when I was paged. Running to the phone, I couldn't imagine who would be paging me. When I answered, I was given a message that would change my life forever. The attorney said that the baby was ours and that we could pick him up at the UCLA Medical Center anytime we were ready. Overwhelmed with excitement and joy, I shared the news with my husband and then with Michelle. She began jumping up and down saying: *I won't have to be all alone anymore.* It had been a very hard two years for all of us, especially for Michelle. She had no way of understanding why her life had changed so dramatically.

The next step was to call my brother and his wife to share our blessing. I asked them to buy some Pampers (diapers) and some Playtex Nursers (bottles) since we were ready to pick up our new baby boy and bring him home with us.

Our holiday was complete and we left early the next day for UCLA to get our son, David. There, I experienced my second cosmic encounter with the mystery of God. David was premature, only four pounds and six ounces. As my husband and I stood in front of the viewing window, I felt and saw a light leaving my heart chakra and I saw a light leave my new, infant son's heart. The two lights met in the center of the hospital nursery and I said aloud, *That's him!* We instantly bonded in that cosmic moment and I never once had any fear that the mother would change her mind. It was six months before the adoption was final. He was my son and I knew no one could ever change that. He is a child of my heart and from the light. David was a blessing to all of us, helping us heal the wound we all had felt so deeply.

Chapter 5

From The Depths Of Despair Into The State Of Ecstasy And Bliss

The death of my son Warren had created a tremendous amount of change within me. And within four years, I found myself dissolving my marriage. This took me into greater growth. I was faced with the fears of being alone and for the very first time I had to take care of myself, as well as, my two children. I wasn't prepared for this extraordinary challenge. Having been married very young, I went from my parents' home right into marriage.

The fears that came up were almost unbearable. The fear of being alone was excruciating. My lowest point came one morning after I sent my children off to school. Very suddenly a movement of agony came up within my body and out of my mouth as I made animal sounds while clawing my fingernails along the wall. I sought out counseling which was my saving grace. I had fallen apart to such a degree that if I hadn't had that one hour weekly session with my counselor, I would have perished. Often, I thought of suicide. It was only the thought of my children needing me that kept me going on. The counselor was a spiritual woman who suggested that I read certain books. The first one that I read was written by Wayne Dyer, which changed the course of my life. As I read, I saw myself in all of my dysfunctional behaviors. It was then that I made a commitment to myself that I would become whole. I hungered to know God, to know love, to be happy and to know peace. The hunger inside of me was so great that I devoured numerous books with their spiritual teachings.

At that time, I didn't realize that a strong intention and a great desire create change or evolution in your life. However, with my strong commitment, I began to evolve.

There was the EST (Erhard Seminars Training) that I attended at the urging of my counselor. She said that I was so stuck in my victimization that I needed to participate in the training. I had no idea what EST entailed, but I followed her guidance and enrolled. This training led to the transformation of my relationship with my father. In one of the processes, I suddenly saw, for the first time that my father was in desperate need of my love and kindness. The next time I saw him, I reached out to him and was able to put my arms around him and love him unconditionally. This was the first time I ever felt this kind of love for him. In that instant, something happened and he felt my love and our relationship changed. We became best friends.

The next step in my evolution was to become involved with the local Church of Religious Science. Here I learned to meditate and twice a week, I attended yoga classes to begin to heal my back. Soon, I became a "workshop junkie" trying everything that came along. I tried rebirthing, breath-work, hypnotherapy, rolfing and Science of Mind I and II. Each of these took me forward, helping me to release my own walls of fear and limitation. My spiritual path consumed me and brought me the first real peace I had ever known.

During these years I developed a fashion consulting business and was very successful. The classes and trainings were paying off. My life as a single woman was fulfilling. I was finally finding myself. I wasn't just a daughter, a mother or a wife. I was creating my own life and loving it. Life was good and I was prospering.

It was during this time that I read Shirley McClaine's book, *Dancing In The Light*, a fascinating work. Shirley introduced me to channeling and an entity called RAMTHA. I distinctly remember saying aloud, *I have to know about this,* and my body felt a rush of energy throughout every single cell. Within a week, I took a friend to church and we visited the bookstore after the service. There on the shelf was a single book entitled, *RAMTHA.* Instantly, I took the book off the shelf, thrilled with my discovery. My friend saw my excitement and said, I'll buy this for you. God was truly working in my life leading me to the next step.

I couldn't wait to begin the adventure of discovering this new information. Reading this material was profound for me. I was unfamiliar with the language Ramtha used, but more importantly, the message was beyond my understanding. I would have to read some of the pages two and three times to get the meaning. But, at a deep level within me, I knew the information was the truth. I recall saying aloud, *This is why I came to life.* I also knew deep within me that this would be my path. I read the book four times in six months and each time I felt that I had never read it before. Each time I was growing in my understanding of the truths contained within the book.

I stopped going to my church, instead I would spend my Sundays alone in my back yard gardening and communing with God. I began to hear messages of truth which brought me greater understanding. I knew I found something precious and I treasured these moments of oneness with God.

After these Sunday experiences, I decided that I needed to find out more about the Ramtha Teachings. I called Ramtha Dialogues in Washington State and found that they would be in the California Desert in December. It would be just around the time of my birthday, a perfect gift. So, I enrolled and off I went, leaving the children with my mother for the five days. I said to her, *I don't know where I am going, but I will never be the same.*

The most significant experience of the week for me was to go out into the desert and find a rock, climb up on the rock and go inside myself in meditation. I can't recall what I said once up on the rock, but suddenly my heart chakra opened. It felt like someone cut my chest open with a knife. What came out was sadness and I just sobbed and sobbed. When I finally stopped, my chest closed and I felt lighter. I climbed down my little mountain and journeyed back to the retreat center.

Something happened up on that rock and I was different. I continued to seek Ramtha messages through video and audio tapes and visited Yelm, Washington for a private audience with the master. It was during this trip that I decided to move to Washington and follow my spiritual path. This was an enormous decision for me. I had lived in my home for twenty years. I had never been separated from my family and friends. Something inside of me, a force that I can't explain even to this day moved me. I sold my home in two weeks and walked away from my prospering business. My daughter, Michelle, age nineteen, refused to join me and I had to leave her behind. My family and friends cried and then became angry with me. There was no support from anyone. Yet, this force inside of me kept moving me on.

The day I left California and began my drive to Yelm, Washington, was the first time I felt fear. As I drove I began to cry. Fear of the unknown had overcome me. My mind was going crazy with doubt, remorse and regret.

I arrived in Yelm and moved into my new home on fifteen acres of land. I had never lived in the country before, nor in a cold climate. My son David was angry with me and resisted finding any good in our new life. I knew no one, had no job and it was very cold. The first morning after arriving, snow was falling and I had to walk out to a shed to carry wood for the wood burning stove so that I could have heat. I cried all the way back to the house. The fashion queen was now carrying wood. I was used to being well coiffured and to wearing designer clothing. My life was certainly different now.

One day, the fear overwhelmed me. After David left for school, I curled up in the fetal position in my bedroom and cried not knowing what to do or where to turn. This experience in Yelm was the second hardest time of my life, yet the most rewarding. My son's death created massive change and now being alone in this rural area and having to face my fears would lead to my transformation. I have found that my hardest times in life have also created the most good. In the moment of the hardships, I could never have imagined where they would take me. I believe now that our hardships bring us closer to God and closer to ourselves. I see them as being in divine order.

I continued to evolve and one day in meditation, I was guided to start a Bed & Breakfast for those coming to hear and see Ramtha teach. There were no hotels in Yelm, just a few diners. There was no flash, no beauty and no fun. But, my Bed & Breakfast was an instant success. Visitors from all over the United States and even from overseas came to be part of the Ramtha work and teachings and stayed with me.

I planted a garden for the first time in my life and enjoyed watching the magic of food growing from seeds. I was such a novice at all of this. Opening the leaves and finding that a cauliflower grows in the center was amazing to me. I was like a child in wonder of nature.

I now realize that in order for me to be reached by Jesus, I had to move out of the structure of my so called "perfect life." I was always on the go and busy, busy, busy. My days were scheduled six months in advance. When I arrived in Yelm, I felt like someone dropped me in the middle of nowhere with no time schedules. Now, I realize that I used to be like a hamster going around and around on a wheel not able to stop. Spirit certainly put a stop to that way of life. There now was plenty of time to be with myself and in nature.

After my encounter with Jesus, he taught me how to become all the things Ramtha talked about. He started me in square one and took me step by step into higher and higher states of consciousness and bliss. He gave me a simple way to master myself. Jesus taught me to master my mind, my emotions and my body. He gave me the truth, the way I had been seeking. The intention and desire I had spoken in my bedroom when I first began my journey was manifesting for me.

I now know the ecstasy of God's love for me. Yes, God brings me to such highs that I literally have orgasmic experiences. The state of bliss is normal and the pleasure of God moving through my body is an every day occurrence. This is available for everyone. It is our natural state. I continue to evolve into the truth. I still continue to heal my limited self through this path of evolution. There is no destination. It is a forever awakening to more love, to more joy, to more self respect, to more self love and to more pleasure.

Chapter 6

The Transition From Channeling

The days of channeling were coming to completion for me. Jesus explained that in order for me to develop as my own Christ Self, *I needed to rely only on the Father within me and not on anything outside myself.* I had begun surrendering my own personal needs and desires through devotion to God as Jesus had suggested. In the first series of Shakti Yoga, postures and prayers are utilized to bring you into a sense of oneness with the Divine. The Shakti Yoga System is a transformational experience of your beliefs or concepts, your emotions, your soul and your cellular structure. Each of the eleven phases has a specific purpose. During this time I was focusing on the initial phase. As I continued to work with these techniques of movement, sound, intentions and prayers, something extraordinary began to happen. At first I felt energy moving throughout my body as a great sense of oneness overcame me. It was a sense of peace I had not known before.

After a few years of facilitating this method to others, however, something profound occurred. One day, as I walked through the grounds of Rosario's Resort on Orcus Island in the Pacific Northwest, I noticed the abundance of wildlife as the deer and fawn were coming to me to eat out of my hand. It was a warm summer day, a perfect outer setting to an inner experience into unknown realms of spirit. I was in the Northwest leading a spiritual retreat. Jesus had requested that I teach in a retreat environment so the participants could be absorbed without distraction in the energy for a period of time. I would teach Yoga in the morning and channel in the afternoon.

On the fifth day when I sat down with my group of retreat participants to begin the Yoga postures and prayers something different happened. Suddenly, while I was in the *Holy Communion* sitting posture, I spontaneously began a singing chant. I don't sing. It was as if it wasn't me. Something overtook me and began to express spiritual wisdom through me as a vehicle. I was in the experience and my ego popped in and said, *What the hell are you doing?* I realized that I had just revealed the most sacred part of myself to others. It was a horrifying feeling. I became overwhelmingly embarrassed. It was as if I were standing naked in front of an entire group. I opened my eyes to see if anyone noticed. Peeking through, I saw that the entire group was apparently enraptured in their own experience of bliss. I was so relieved. But in my head, I asked Jesus, what is going on? He replied, *The Father was speaking through you as you.* I had become my Spirit.

This experience of allowing Spirit to express through me has continued. It is truly a state of bliss. In these moments, I feel complete with no needs or wants.

A year then passed. Sitting on my patio in the desert of Southern California, sunbathing in 'my office', my favorite place, I had an over-whelming sense of how wonderful my life had become. I was comfortable and quite content. And then I heard His voice. Jesus said, *It is time to move to the Big Island of Hawaii and expand. Take nothing with you.* I thought Hawaii and expanding sounded really good. I moved.

I had heard that Hawaii can purge you, especially the Big Island where legends of *Pele* become reality. I found them to be real. *Pele* is the great Goddess of Transformation, and so it was for me. The change from the Southern California environment of Country Club living and malls contrasted sharply with remoteness and simplicity of island living. There were few shops and fewer distractions. In the beginning, I found myself homesick and wanted to know *when can I leave?* I was told that I had to stay a year. It was an adjustment for me. When I settled in, however, I found that I could sit on the beach for hours and just 'be'. The pace was slow and I found myself not as motivated as before. I could see the differences in energy and consciousness in an environment obsessed with business, money, personal appearance and hectic schedules as compared to a life of just living. I grew to discover the joy of letting go especially of my personal image.

Shortly after settling into life on the Big Island of Hawaii, I found myself leading another retreat at Kalani Honua Conference Center in the rain-forest. It was May of 1993 and the air was warm and balmy. Walking across the grounds to the *hale* (Hawaiian for house), Jesus again spoke to me informing me that I would not channel at this retreat. *What am I supposed to do with all these people for seven days*, I asked. He replied, *Lie down and everything will come from within you. You are ready to teach.* This was no comfort to me. Instead, it felt more like a bomb had just been dropped on me.

I took a deep breath and walked into the *hale* where twenty-six partici-pants from all over the US and Canada had gathered to hear Jesus' pro-found wisdom. While the group sat on their yoga mats and waited, I stood up and announced what had just occurred while walking across the lawn. Fortunately, they were all very supportive, wondering what would happen next. I too wondered what would happen next.

Feeling like I had no choice, I obeyed and laid down. I was so stunned from what had just happened, I couldn't even begin to imagine what was about to occur. There wasn't time to think, so I began the postures and prayers of Shakti Yoga. To my amazement, the energy began to move my body so profoundly that my legs were bouncing rapidly up and down in what I later learned is called a *kriya*. A *kriya* is an involuntary response or movement. As the light (energy) moves through the body, it hits blockages in the energy channels which causes the body to jerk or twitch. Then, my abdominal muscles began to contract as if in childbirth. It felt like I was being consumed by the light of God. With this movement, a breath began to breathe me. The energy moved up my spine through my chakras (vortexes of energy located in the subtle body) and out the top of my head. With this, I went into a state of ecstasy. It was as if the divine energy was making love to me within, caressing and bringing me to higher and higher states of ecstasy. This energy felt very sensual and orgasmic in nature. This phenomena went on for the full seven days. It didn't occur all at once however. The experiences gradually intensified and built over the week.

During this incredible week, infinite wisdom seemed to effortlessly come forth from some previously unknown part of me. I had never heard this information before. The knowledge of *Sacred Seals* and information on activating the brain just came forth as it was occurring for me and the group. Jesus has told me that this experience is the birthing of the Christ Light within. It has since happened to many while practicing Shakti Yoga or during a Shakti Therapy session.

It was a totally outrageous week. During many of the yoga sessions, states of ecstasy apparently overtook various members of the group. It may have sounded as though we were having an orgy. This energy pouring en mass through the group created orgasmic sensations for everyone. In the next *hale,* another workshop was in session. They heard these sounds of ecstasy coming from our hale and at lunch they jokingly invited themselves to join our group saying they wanted whatever we had. None believed that our sounds were in response to praying.

I myself felt in awe of what was happening. I had never dreamed I could experience so much pleasure and bliss in the physical by praying, much less an entire room filled with people experiencing the same thing. I have realized since this retreat that the human body is created to experience pleasure and not pain and this is the value of relying on the Father-Mother Presence within me.

A Teaching From Jesus On The Sacred Seals

You are not truly living until you activate the life of God within. You will then live in alignment with God's laws.

Through my process of activating the sacred seals within me, I have found the Kingdom of Heaven, my divinity in each chakra. The **Sacred Seals** are located in the center of each chakra. They are chambers of energy lying dormant waiting to be birthed into life. Within each sacred seal is an aspect of your divinity and each has a divine purpose. Once you activate the divinity that is sealed within the chakras, one by one, it is as if you have a new computer. This computer is within you and it is operated by your thoughts, prayers, sounds and feelings which bring forth your grace, beauty, power, knowledge, love and more, all from within. Essentially, it is all that you need in any given moment. God is alive within you waiting to be experienced and expressed in this dimension. As this new foundation is developed and solidified, you hold a new vibration within you. Currents and waves of energy are released from the first seal sending out a new energy flow which affects the entire system. These waves of electrical energy are sent up the central nervous system to activate the brain which can bring about full enlightenment. Also, these new currents and waves of energy develop and expand the DNA system. Once the sacred seals begin the activating process, you are creating a new foundation for your life, the foundation of a Christ or a fully realized being. The energy of the Divine Mother within you (your Shakti) begins to heal you. The Mother knows exactly what is next in your path to enlightenment and you just need to ask. She begins to transform the distorted energy to return you to balance, love and light.

Wisdom From Jesus On The Sacred Seals

Greetings, Beloved of God,

Stand in the pureness of your tears, of your sadness, the pureness of your anger and fears, for through this shall come the pureness of your love. The gateway to your spiritual body is through your emotional body, beloved ones. You and only you can open the doorways that are barred shut within. Behind these doorways lie your great sadness. This sadness is your passageway to your spiritual body, to your supreme love, to the supreme God that lies within you waiting to be birthed.

You have been crying out for assistance. You cry out for your God powers. **These qualities of God's powers are needed now on your plane to restore balance and harmony, first to you and through you to the world.** *There are many that are ready to activate the power of God that lies dormant within them. There are those whose intentions are pure, their service to God and humanity is great. These beloved ones shall not abuse this power. Now is the time for you to be given the power of the God that lies dormant within you.*

My beloved ones, **within your Sacred Seals lies dormant a great energy. It is your power. The Glory of God resides within your Sacred Seals. As each seal is activated, the God-Goddess within the seal becomes a live embodiment within you. Once, all seven of your Sacred Seals are fully activated and releasing their specific energies, you will have the power to manifest in your kingdom, in the moment exactly what you desire. Each seal releases a current of energy unique unto itself upon your command to bring forth manifestation. This energy of God is lying dormant within each seal waiting to come to life, to live through you.**

It is as on a cloudy day. There is darkness. It is dreary. It is dismal. You know that the power of the sun does exist, however, it is not felt or seen in the moment. You are lost in the fog, lost in the storm, and yet, in your awareness, you remember the life qualities of the sun. You do not have the power to command the sun to bring forth its life-giving radiance.

There is within each seal, the power of the sun waiting to come to life, to clear from your body, emotions and mind, the storm of anger, to clear the dark clouds of sadness. Once the activation begins, the power of the Golden Sun within the Sacred Seals begins to clear the atmosphere, your body, mind and emotions. As you clear the storm within, the power of God, the Golden Sun in each seal becomes stronger and stronger until it is pulsating life through you.

And one fine day, beloved ones, you will stand strong and tall. You will put forth your intent and so it shall be. Each Sacred Seal will bring forth the precise energies needed for manifestation. You will indeed be powerful and be aligned to God's will for you.

I bring you the gift of activating your Sacred Seals. Look within, feel and know if you are indeed aligned to the evolution of life. Are you aligned in service? Is your intent pure? If you are indeed aligned and your service is pure, then come forth for the activation of your Sacred Seals. It is time that this God power be present upon your plane. There is a need in the density of your dimension for the power that is within you to be activated.

It is within you. You have been told this for eons and now you are being given the gift of activation that which is within. And so it is. Amen

Your brother in service,
Jesus of Nazareth

Chapter 7

An Experience of the Activation of the First and Second Sacred Seals

In September of 1997, a student of mine came for a Shakti Therapy session and during that session, the Divine Mother within me said that this was to be the day to activate her first and second sacred seals. I was given the prayers to bring forth her divine Christ light into life. Here is her description.

The activating of my seals was a divine experience and my words will not do justice. With a full and grateful heart, I will attempt to convey it.

Prior to this experience, I had been practicing Shakti Yoga for about a month. Each practice was unique in that more and different energy would vibrate through my body bringing with it a new awakening each time.

When I say vibrate through my body, I mean a movement that my conscious mind had not initiated. Perhaps, the shaking of an arm or leg that leads to the abdomen and up the spine and out of my body. This is a divine feeling and always leads me into peace.

This particular day, I did my yoga practice and then went to receive a healing session with Virginia. When I got on the healing table, Virginia shared that this was to be the day for activating my first and second seals. I was excited, thrilled, honored and there was the doubt that it might not happen. All this was swirling around in my mind as the session began. At first, I could only feel the incredible warmth and love energy coming through Virginia. Then, I remember being shown my own internal/external light. (That flame of energy held deeply within us all that always is.) My breathing became spontaneous as if in labor. Many times my body moved and shook rapidly. The light became so bright at this point that it held me in a 360 degree egg and it showered through every cell in my body. After this, there was a time of bliss as I have not known before. As the breathing and movement continued, it became more intense calling forth a powerful energy within my womb—but what? This, for me, was the experience of birthing and being "The Divine Mother". At this point, I asked for the help of Jesus Christ and immediately he was in front of me. He put his arms around me and held me. He showed me that he lives within me, that he lives within us all. We are all actually what is meant by the "second coming of Christ." It is within us, held in our bodies and our hearts.

My own birth of the Christ light occurred in 1993 in a retreat setting. Today, the birthing and activation of the Christ light is available to all those who are ready to receive it.

The Divinity Of The Chakras

I would like to share with you the divinity of the chakra system. The chakras are more than vortexes of energy. Within each chakra lies the divine male and female aspects of God that have been lying dormant inside each one of us. This is where the power of God lies, where the transformational energy for healing lies, where the wisdom and knowledge of God lies. There is a divine purpose and function for each chakra. The divinity within each chakra is the vehicle to activate the brain for full enlightenment and to expand the DNA system. It is the power and glory of the Christ, the Kingdom of God within.

THE FIRST CHAKRA

Location: Base of the Spine
Color: Red
Divinity: Female Aspect—The Mother of Creation
Function—the flow of inspiration and divine ideas

Male Aspect—The Passion to Manifest
Function—the passion to manifest and fully live your creation; to put the inspiration and divine ideas into action

The first chakra is the life force center. When this Sacred Seal is activated, you will find the Eternal Flame within it. After activation, the color becomes a fiery red and begins to burn away the old, limited consciousness within the cells and energy moves up through your central nervous system into the brain to activate and awaken it.

THE SECOND CHAKRA

Location: Midway between the pubis and the navel
Color: Orange
Divinity: Female Aspect—The Divine Mother
              Function—to transform energy

              Male Aspect—The Beloved Father
              Function—to protect, to provide for, to bring wisdom
              and guidance

This chakra is the transformation center and when this Sacred Seal is activated, you will have the power to transform your energy, thoughts, emotions and physical body. As you come home to the Mother and bring your feelings and issues to Her, She transforms them through love. In this Sacred Seal, there is a pyramid in the shape of a womb in both men and women. This is known as The Womb of Mankind. Transformation occurs within this womb. New energy is sent up through the pathways to every cell in your body transforming them from density into light.

THE THIRD CHAKRA

Location: Between the navel and the base of the sternum
Color: Yellow
Divinity: Female Aspect—The Desire of the Goddess
              Function—to desire and ignite the flame of God's will

              Male Aspect—The Will of God
              Function—to bring the desire into form

The third chakra is the generating center. The Goddess in you does the desiring. If the desire is burning in Her, then She ignites the Will of God and He generates this desire into form quickly. The function of the male is to serve the female. He serves her through honoring her desire and bringing it into form.

THE FOURTH CHAKRA

Location: Center of the chest (Heart Center)
Colors: Green (healing) Pink (self-love) Gold (divine love)
Divinity: Female Aspect—The Queen
              Function—to reign in Her Kingdom

              Male Aspect—The King
              Function—to have dominion over life

This is the center of living in the Kingdom. When you are LIVING IN THE KINGDOM, you are enjoying life with no lack, no worry, no doubt and no needs. You are then living whatever your heart desires. This is JOY, the paradise of emotions. When the lower centers are each in balance, you live in joy. In the first center, the male creates his domain through passion to live the female's creation. He does what he needs to do to put it into form. In the second center, while the womb is transforming the emotions and issues, he is providing protection and caring for the physical needs of the feminine. He is giving the guidance that you need to move forward in your emotions and issues. In the third center, he is honoring your feelings, desires, wishes and needs. Having done all of this, he has provided the domain in which the female can reign in JOY.

THE FIFTH CHAKRA

Location: At the throat
Color: Blue
Divinity: Female Aspect—The Priestess
              Function—fearlessness
              Male Aspect—The Priest
              Function—speaking the truth

This center is the state of deliverance, a state in which all things are possible and delivered to your doorstep. **Everything already is in the fifth**

center. It is exciting because your first four chakras are in balance and your creative idea is now delivered to you. Your feminine aspect has already had the creative thought, you have transformed the fear or doubt about it, you have desired and emotionally felt it. In your heart, you are living the joy of the idea. Now, because you are living the joy of the idea, it will be delivered to you. Your male aspect has done whatever he needed to do. He has provided the passion to manifest the feminine creation, protected, cared for and guided you through the transformational time. In the third center, he has honored your desires and in the fourth center, he has created a domain for you to experience the joy of life. Therefore, he could **speak the truth** about any of the former, saying whatever is needed for you.

THE SIXTH CHAKRA

Location: Middle of the forehead
Color: All colors, all hues—(it is the blending of all that you are. It
             is the evolution of your soul coming into physical form)
Divinity: Female Aspect—The Maiden
             Function—to be pure in body, mind and soul

             Male Aspect—The Knight
             Function—to live in honor

In this center, honor returns to us. The Knight lives by a code of honor. He knows what correct action is and lives accordingly. The Knight is the law-giver in his kingdom and lives according to his laws, honoring the Maiden and protecting her purity. As the Knight in you develops, you become the conqueror of your kingdom. When the Sixth Sacred Seal is activated, you begin to live as a true mystic. At this level of spiritual evolution, there is no longer a veil and you will be able to see clearly. You must be extremely healed, otherwise you would not be able to stand the pain of what you see in the souls of humanity.

THE SEVENTH CHAKRA

Location: Crown of the head
Color: Purple and lavender hues representing royalty.
               White light representing Divinity as a Human God.
Divinity: Female Aspect—Pure Divine Love
               Function—to be the Noble Love of God

               Male Aspect—Pure Divine Light
               Function—to be the Noble Light of God

This Seal (chakra) is also known as the KNOWINGNESS CENTER. You are a noble being. To be noble means: TO KNOW YOU ARE GOD: to know who you are and to live in the truth without limitations. You have resurrected your consciousness and live in the Noble Mind of God. In this state of noble consciousness, you experience oneness and equality between the male and female aspects of God within. There is no gender in this state of being. You are Pure Love and Light, Pure God/Human. You know you are ENTITLED to live in the abundance of God's Kingdom.

Chapter 8

My Seven Years of Mystery Training with Jesus

When I agreed to be a channel for this work that Jesus ask me to deliver through me to humanity, he requested seven years of my life. He said that it would take seven years of purification for me to begin to hold the Christ vibration. I accepted this mission, which he calls, A Mission in Truth, bringing the truth of God to humanity.

These seven years were like living in a monastery, very different from the life I had known before, but normal for a mystery school. There were no books, no television, no newspapers, no normal relationships with males and no outside interference from the world. Everything would have to come from the God within me. I was to rely on God and become as God Is. I was challenged and tested over and over again as I continued to dissolve the ego. With time, I began to feel more deeply not only my deepest sorrow, but also the joy of my own Essence. (Today, I feel as if my body is a highly fine-tuned instrument and that it is being played constantly as I feel the light moving throughout my entire being. Whenever anything is said or done to me or to someone in my presence, I feel the pleasure or pain of the intent behind the words or actions.)

Throughout these years, I lived very isolated from society and I was consumed with the project of the transformation of my body, mind and emotions. I didn't have a community to interact with. I didn't join in or participate with others in classes because I was traveling two weekends per month doing channelings and classes. When I was home, I was preparing for the next trip and healing myself, which was my major project. I had to attain the new information and cellularly embrace it before I could teach the next phase of mastery. There was no time to create a life in the community where I lived.

The finale of these seven years was a retreat in Hawaii over New Year's Eve. The name I was given for the retreat was, *The Feast of the Passover,* which Jesus says means passing from the material plane into the spiritual plane.

Each day that I lead the Shakti Yoga, my vibration would continue to increase. I became very ill with a high fever, head congestion and I had difficulty eliminating fluids from my body. Jesus said these symptoms would last ten days because I had begun to embody the Christ vibration and major purification was occurring. And in ten days, I was completely healed of all discomfort and symptoms of illness. The amazing part about these highly transformational experiences was that when I was teaching, I would have no symptoms of illness. My body was sustained by the light within me. As soon as I was finished teaching the session, I again became overwhelmingly ill and returned to bed until the next session. This miracle occurred over and over during the retreat.

I finally finished my seven year commitment with Jesus. Now, I could have my life back. I went on strike. No more teaching. I was free to attend a local church, take yoga classes, enjoy church retreats and develop friends in the community. I loved my new freedoms especially being a student and no responsibilities. I had *"a life"*, but I didn't know what I wanted to do, So, my money was running out.

Chapter 9

The Foundation for the Rest of My Life

One day while in yoga class, a voice (my inner child) said: *Let's go to yoga camp.* Immediately after class I went to buy a Yoga Journal. What I found was that there were dozens of yoga schools offering certification programs. So, I decided to get certified while learning more about other forms of yoga. I chose a school that two of my Shakti Yoga students had attended. The time was right and I just needed the money.

Jesus said that this time at yoga camp would be the foundation for the rest of my life. This intrigued me. He never explains these comments. This left me to find out through experience what he was talking about. He also told me that I would have the money, approximately three thousand dollars, for the month long yoga training.

Time was growing close and I didn't have the money. I called my uncle to wish him a "Happy Birthday." To my surprise he said, I hear you want to go to school. *Yes*, I replied, *but I don't have the funds yet.* It's in the mail, was his answer. Thanking him for his support, I began to cry. *That's what uncles are for,* was his reply.

I put all of my belongings into storage and off I went into this adventure. I found the work interesting since I had never been exposed to a *guru* or Indian philosophy. I enjoyed learning their traditions and about their religion. Chanting was enjoyable as well as learning more about the *asanas* or postures. Classes were held seven days a week from 7 a.m. until 5 p.m. with evening sessions as well. I was used to being disciplined, so the demanding schedule didn't bother me. However, after two weeks of Sanskrit, I was hitting a wall of resistance. I longed for the sweetness of praying and toning with my Shakti Yoga and the bliss it brings me. That morning during the yoga class, I kept hearing, *Do not put false gods before you.* So, I began sounding with my *asanas* and saying my prayers from the heart. Later in the morning, we were working with a partner assisting each other in the *fish asanas*. I worked with my partner, assisting her and when my turn came, I told her: *I have to do this my way.* I then said my prayer of surrender and my body spontaneously began to move into the fish posture, then back down and I began to bounce several inches off the ground as the energy of the prayer moved through me. This had happened before, but my partner had never seen or felt anything like this. The instructors were amazed at the Shakti or Holy Spirit moving through me.

After lunch there was a period of chanting and this day we were to chant the *Hare Krishna* Chant. I decided to say Christ and chant to Christ. Fifteen minutes into the session, I allowed the Holy Spirit to take full sway of my body. It took over, moving through me and I felt great pleasure. Suddenly, from deep inside of my gut (third chakra), my voice said, *Lord Jesus, you are my Lord and my God and I will only follow you.* Tears streamed down my face. My body began to vibrate at a frequency so high that it took me into full orgasm, releasing the sounds of ecstasy. The energy moved from my first chakra up through my body and chakra system, out the crown of my head whipping my body back and forth as if I were a rag doll. Upon completion of the movement, I fell exhausted to the floor. Then, I realized what had happened as seventy students and our instructors were looking at me shocked and wondering what that was all about. I pulled myself up from the floor, embarrassed and yet so filled with bliss that it really didn't matter that they didn't understand the mysteries of God moving through the human form.

Even though I had worked with Jesus as my teacher and guide, I had never surrendered to him. A part of me, my ego, always held back wanting to be in control, wanting life my way rather than God's divine will for me. When I proclaimed him as my Lord and my God, I surrendered my life and my allegiance to him and to following my divine path to completion. I had finally surrendered to fulfilling my mission.

After that moment, Jesus again manifested and spoke to me for the remaining two weeks of my training. **He told me that I was to write a book and share the Shakti Yoga with the world. This yoga was a vehicle to birth forth the light of God within humanity and that it was part of the movement of the Second Coming of Christ. Jesus said that the light that would be ignited and birthed within humanity was the Christ light and that Shakti Yoga was a way to ignite that light. He also told me that when enough of us have become the vibration of the Christ, he would come again. Jesus went on to say that we are the Second Coming and that Christ resides in all of us.**

I completed the month-long training for the certification program and it was time for my final test where I was to lead yoga to a group of other students as a teacher observed and graded me. The night before my final, my stomach was in knots and I couldn't sleep. In a healing that I did on myself, I discovered that my stomach was in knots because I couldn't be out of integrity. I felt that it was impossible for me to lead the yoga as I had been trained in for the past four weeks. So I decided to teach from my truth, teaching what I knew within me was the truth. I also decided that I was willing to fail my final test and leave without a yoga teaching certificate. I would leave with my self respect and my knowing what was right for me. To me, no compromise was acceptable.

As I was teaching my fellow students in practice sessions, my body would go into spontaneous *kriya* as the Holy Spirit moved through me. The instructors found this unusual and they probably were frightened by the movements. One or two of them would try to stop me from my experience by placing their hands on my shoulder or knee and ask me to be still.

For the final test. I was the last one in my group to lead. When my turn came I lead the yoga from within me, speaking wisdom about each posture. This was not part of the program that I was training in. When I had completed leading the students, my grading instructor said to me, *A good teacher knows her material, a great teacher knows her material and teaches from within herself and you are a great teacher.* To my amazement, I passed. My grading instructor asked me how long I had been teaching. I told her and shared that I also had a video tape of my Shakti Yoga, which she later purchased. God had sent me the perfect grading instructor, one who resonated with the energy I represented.

Now, I was to begin my *mission in truth.* I was guided to go to Hawaii and teach. While there, I stayed with Rosalina, who was the first person I had certified to teach Shakti Yoga. I shared my mission with her and she agreed to assist me. We were walking on Kailua Beach, which was our favorite. The water was turquoise and many shades of blue that day. As we walked and talked, I remember saying, *Well, I have no money and no resources to begin writing a book and starting a school. It's going to be interesting to see how this all unfolds.* I saw this project as a great adventure into God's plan for me.

I returned to California to visit with family. One day while doing my Shakti Yoga meditation, I ask Jesus where I should live. He replied that I should return to the California Desert. Then, I asked him, how to do this, since, I only had one hundred dollars to my name. Again, I received a answer: *You will stay with Mary.* Mary was a young woman I had met at a church retreat just before leaving the desert. We had a instant connection and I had also done a healing on Mary after the retreat. During the healing Jesus merged with us and he became a large part of Mary's healing and life.

As soon as I received the message from Jesus about staying with Mary Dann, *I* called her. Her words to me were:*I redecorated the guest room. The key is waiting for you and you can stay as long as you like.*

I was blessed again with God's love and a home to live in and a sister on the same path as I was, a path into God's Kingdom.

I began to establish myself doing healings at a spiritual resort & health center and teaching yoga classes. I also returned to my church. One evening after a church meditation, I shared with the group my mission of writing a yoga book. A artist friend who was there, volunteered to do the art work for my book as a gift to me. We began the project and he also told me that there was an apartment in his complex available for rent. At that time, I wasn't financially prepared to move, however, I looked at the apartment where he was manager and it was quite adorable. But, I had to say, *Not at this time*, and thanked him for considering me.

One month later, Mary decided to move to the Los Angeles area and I went off to lead a Yoga Certification Program in Hawaii. While I was doing my yoga, God told me to call John, the apartment manager and let him know that I would take the adorable apartment that he showed me. It had been six weeks since he showed the apartment to me and the likelihood of it still being available was not good. It was winter season in the desert and the most desirable time to be there. When I called, John still had the apartment available. Again, I was invited to move in with no credit check, just sending a small deposit. I returned home and as Mary made her move, so did I. However, I was faced with the challenge of tripling my income to meet my expenses.

After moving into the apartment, I was guided to give notice at work and to do all my work out of my home. I was petrified as I gave my notice. That evening, I began to do my Shakti Yoga and pray. I asked God to take the fear out of my body so that I could follow my path. God took it away. Each day of that first month was an adventure into God's abundant life. The phone would ring and I would be asked to do a massage or a healing. Somehow, I created enough to meet my new expenses.

Two years later I was leading an evening workshop in January 1999 called *NEW BEGINNINGS*. The class was on manifestation: to live this new year co-creating our lives as we choose. Near the end of the workshop, I lead the group into proclaiming their truths and desires. This was a process of accepting the truth from the soul. From within me came a prayer and declaration saying, ***I am ready to take my work into the mainstream.*** I had never consciously thought or said this before.

Five days later I received an astonishing phone call from a friend who I had not seen in nearly five years. She told me that she would be coming to the desert for some rest and would I be available to have lunch with her. The following week at lunch we visited and I also arranged to have a dinner party for Cheryl and several other friends that knew me from my earlier channeling days.

Cheryl had attended my channeling debut with Jesus eleven years previous. We were old friends and she was also the person who invited me to channel Jesus in Hawaii where she had a home. After dinner, we were all chatting and Cheryl said, *I want to help you with your book. My husband of four years is the Founder of one of the largest literary agencies in the country.* At the time, I didn't even know there were literary agents. However, soon I had an agent and my book would now become a reality. I then began the project of getting my book ready for publishing.

It was now spring and Jesus once again guided me to give up my home ***to go and be among the people.*** I put everything into storage at the end of April with no plans for the Summer or Fall. To my awe, God sent me many invitations to speak and teach all across the nation from California to South Carolina.

I don't know where I am going from this point on. However, I do know that my life is with God and I have no life separate from God.

Three Stages of Shakti Yoga

Whatever You Are Devoted to You Become

Surrender
Through
Devotion

The Truth Shall Set You Free

Acceptance
The Law
of
Acceptance

Mastery
You have
become the
living word of
God

The Power To Manifest

Chapter 10

Your Development With Shakti Yoga

As you practice Shakti Yoga, you will develop your ability to focus and be in the moment fully experiencing and living the truth in the now. You will learn to live whatever emotion, whatever truth is there in the moment; be it love, joy, peace, sadness or pain. With consistent practice, you will learn that you can move easily from the darkness into the light by being real and living the truth in each moment, no longer resisting the darkness, but choosing to surrender into the darkness. Trust will be developed. You will begin to trust the Divine source within you to bring forth the perfect prayers for you. The ego mind of doubt and judgment will begin to dissolve as you speak the words of truth and love. The God of your being will begin to speak through you, as you.

As you begin to speak to God, speaking the prayers outlined in this book, remember to be in the moment and above all-BE REAL. The prayers I offer to you are a guide. Your development is based upon speaking the truth, being vulnerable, sincere and honest. Each time you lie down to begin your Shakti Yoga (which is speaking directly to the God within you), your prayers will have their own life and pattern. Let yourself unfold naturally by speaking what is in your heart and soul in the moment.

Chapter 11

The Phenomenon Of Activating Your Sacred Seals

Your sacred seals will activate and you will be purified in body, mind, soul and emotions. The Divine Mother energy within will cleanse you of your pains, guilt, shame and karma. You will begin to purify and your healing will take its own course, directed by the Mother. Your healing will be cellular, very deep and very profound.

As your sacred seals activate and grow in strength, your body will go through many changes. You will truly have a physical and energetic phenomenon occur within your physical body.

The light of God is electrical and it will electrify your physical body. During this electrifying experience of your sacred seals activating, you may experience the following:

* Your head may be moved back by a force of energy from within you. It may feel as if it is pinned back and you are unable to move it. This is the state of surrender where you are physically surrendering your body to the God within.

* Your chest may also be arched and held up by the energy for a period of time. Remember, you have surrendered to the force within and are not in control here.

* For both men and women, the muscles in your second chakra area will begin to spontaneously contract as in a birthing experience. This is the Divine Mother energy birthing the light within.

* A spontaneous breath will begin to breathe through you moving the energy up the chakra system and out the top of your head clearing blockages as it moves through you. While you are moving through these blockages, you may experience states of pleasure (heaven) and pain (hell). In one moment, you may feel the ecstasy and bliss of the light of God tingling and caressing every cell of your body and in the next moment, you may hit a blockage and feel the pain of an experience stored in the soul record of your body. You may even have a flashback and view the experience as it is being dissolved by the light.

This phenomenon of awakening and activating your sacred seals or the Divine Mother energy may last about thirty minutes where the body is continually moving in and out of states of pleasure and pain. Spontaneous surrender postures and breathing will continue through-out this time. The pleasure of the Divine Mother energy may heighten and you may find yourself making sounds of ecstasy as in love making. The senses are being awakened and purified as the body is being cleared of past experiences.

Upon completion of this birthing process, every cell in your body will be alive with God's Life. You will feel more sensual than ever before. A sensual being is one that is alive, awake, illuminated with light, sensitive to life, to self and to God.

This is a very natural, mystical experience with your own Divine Nature. All of this Divine mystery occurs as a result of our devotion to God, our willingness to surrender to God and into our own darkness, and our great willingness to trust God throughout this whole process.

Chapter 12

The Science of the Body

Shakti Yoga is based on the science of the body as Jesus brought it to me. Begin to think of everything as vibration rather than good and bad, or right and wrong. We are drawn to people, places and things through vibration. We attract to us people and experiences by the vibrations that we send out to the world.

Thought is electrical and vibrates at its own frequency.
Vibrations are the language of God.

In other dimensions, communication occurs through sound, color and symbols. These are other ways of transmitting vibrations. They all hold consciousness and vibrate the frequency of consciousness through the sound, the color or the symbol. We communicate consciousness through the spoken word, through art, writing, music, dance and movement here in this dimension.

Your body lives within its own atmosphere of thought, which is your electrical field or aura. Beyond your aura, which is filled with color, is a pure energy or white light which is your spirit. Your spirit is one with the Mind of God. The Mind of God knows all there is to know. Superconsciousness is one-mindedness (the Infinite Mind of God).

Your spirit brings you electrical impulses from the Mind of God. What you think determines which impulses will come to you. You draw to you vibrations to match your thoughts or frequencies. In Shakti Yoga, we tap into the Infinite Mind which brings us high frequencies. These frequencies then begin to purify the atmosphere around you, your body and your soul. The atmosphere around your body is made up of vibrations from both your conscious and unconscious thoughts. This atmosphere is a reflection of your attitudes of life, of yourself and of others.

Your body holds the past in it. It holds the vibrations of the material plane which are your human appetites for pleasure. Jesus says, ***If you choose to pleasure your body (your animal soul), you will know all of the pains of hell.*** This statement refers to all of our human appetites for instant pleasure, such as drugs, cigarettes, alcohol, food, money and sex. It is when we are addicted and at the affect of the addiction that we know the pains of hell. We have the opportunity to dissolve the addictions and their vibrations in Shakti Yoga.

The River Of Consciousness

There is a river of consciousness that feeds you. It is the river of life force energy that flows through the central nervous system to support life in every cell of your body. Your consciousness creates and conducts the flow of this life force energy.

You send back to the Mind of God the frequencies of the thoughts that you have embraced through your soul. When you live in service to God, your soul releases power and love (higher frequencies). If you choose to serve the mind of the body, the material plane, you send back to the Mind of God a lower frequency.

Each thought that you hold has a different frequency and vibrates at its own rate. The purer the thought, the higher the frequency. Jesus says: *When you are pure in thought, you are one with God.*

Everything that you think and feel affects every cell in your body. It also affects the river of consciousness that feeds everyone. You are very important and powerful. Your thoughts can purify the planet or contaminate it because every thought goes into the river of consciousness. Once a thought is felt and sent out through your soul, it is available for everyone and everything.

In nature, you are fed by the vibrations of purity, of life and of God and it is easier to connect with your spirit and the Infinite Mind of God. In a church or temple, you will also find vibrations of peace and love. In your own home, you can begin to build an energy of love and devotion to God by setting aside a room or area in which to practice your Shakti Yoga and meditations. Use the same space each time you engage in the yoga and meditation practice and the vibrations will become purer.

This principle is also true in reverse. When you enter a place of lower vibrations, such as a large city or in a bar, you are polluting your energy field and are being fed lower vibrations. This will affect your entire being, your mental and emotional state, which in turn affects the chemical flow of your body.

How Your Thoughts Affect Your Body

Your brain is both a receiver and transmitter of vibration. When you receive a thought, the frequency of the thought is amplified by the pineal gland and shot through the central nervous system to every nerve ending and cell in the body. The pituitary and pineal glands secrete hormones according to the vibrations they receive from the thought. Your thoughts and their frequencies govern your entire body chemistry.

In Shakti Yoga, you hold, focus on and embrace pure thoughts which create higher frequency vibrations in your body. When you reach these higher frequencies, your brain begins to activate, your sacred seals begin to activate and the *kundalini* will flow freely.

Your thoughts become part of every cell in your body. When you embrace a thought emotionally, it is stored in the cells and becomes the mind of the body. As you embrace the higher vibrations of truth, your flesh becomes purified and vibrates at a higher frequency. Illumination then occurs in the flesh and a radiant light emanates from within you.

A MESSAGE FROM JESUS ON THE SCIENCE OF THE BODY
(Becoming a Christ, God's Ideal of Man)

First, you must have faith, believing that God is within you and that this Source of Power can create all things that you need to take you forward on your journey into Christhood.

Bless the Father within and give thanks to the beloved God within you for all your good. By loving and blessing the Father within, you become the God that is within you, for whatever you are focusing on, multiplies. In this way you accept the truth. You experience the Father within and what you experience becomes knowledge within you. You become God-realized, a Christ. God is then in every cell of your body.

As you meditate, enter into the state of holy communion, which is receiving the vibrations of love, wisdom and guidance from your own divine essence. Your brain receives the frequencies of this truth through your spirit. The brain then sends impulses of these vibrations to the body through the central nervous system. Your body will begin to vibrate and even quake from these vibrations because each nerve ending is receiving the electrical shock of a high voltage of energy. This begins to ascend the density of your physical body form into light, love and joy.

As the cells receive the impulses of divine thought through energy, this divine energy is projected into every cell of your body. This is created when the divine energy in the cells multiplies itself

Each organ of your body is an amplifying center for these holy thoughts of truth. When each organ is vibrating and amplifying the truth, there is great harmony in the body. You then stand and have dominion over your life. Then, you have brought forth the Holy Spirit into creative action. The soul and the body become one force, one power and one God (wholeness). You then stand as supreme man, an all powerful Christ.

First, you must have the desire to become the supreme, powerful man. Then, have a great desire to move your will into action. The greater your desire, the more powerful your will becomes, for desire is needed to add the spark of life to your will. When there is great harmony between your will and your desire, then your will springs forth and its command is brought forth immediately into life.

Your brother in service
Jesus of Nazareth

Chapter 13

The Aum

The *aum* is an attempt to reproduce the sounds of creation. As you sound the *aum*, you become one with the mystical tones of the universe. Mystical sounds have the ability to change the frequency of our bodies. Everything that comes into form in our dimension comes in on a sound wave, as well as, a light wave. Sound and light are one and they work together in harmony.

In the practice of Shakti Yoga, the aum will assist you in moving the energy through the body. As you sound aum, you will be releasing blockages from the body. A very pure sound can penetrate through matter rearranging the molecules and atoms. You will become purer and clearer as you continue to practice Shakti Yoga, so your sounding will become more effective and profound. Remember the biblical story of the walls of Jericho crumbling from the pure sounds, or the pure tones of a soprano breaking glass.

When I first started channeling for audiences, I would go into prayer and meditation in preparation for Jesus to enter my being. He would be standing on my right side waiting, asking me to sound. I didn't sing and had frequently been criticized as a child for singing "off key." Instantly, I replied *no!* He would calmly and firmly say, *open your mouth and sound.* Again, I would say—*No, I don't sing.* While the audience patiently waited,

I continued my resistant dialogue with Jesus. With kindness and firmness, he persisted in his requests to have me sound. Finally, I would agree and open my mouth. As I sounded, I found that the fear left my body and my frequency would begin to lighten until my ego could step aside and allow Jesus in. Hopefully, you won't have to be as resistant as I was to using sound.

A nurse in one on my classes brought to my attention that sounding the *aum* is a bodily release. Bodily releases occur naturally when the atoms of the body are overstressed and out of balance. Then, the body makes the adjustments through an arf, which may be a hiccup, sneeze, cough, belch, passing wind, etc. This arf is an attempt to bring balance back to the body. When we sound aum, the same process of returning balance to the body at the atomic level occurs.

Meaning of the AUM

A—Awakening of the God Within
U—Unification with the Christ Within
M-Mastery-God I AM

THE AUM EXERCISE

Bring your attention and awareness down to the second chakra. Contract the muscles of your abdomen pushing them toward your spine. As you do so, let the sound of the A come forth from within you. Feel it as it resonates in your body tuning your cells to the sound of A awakening the God (Shakti) within. Another way to awaken the God within is by singing. Jesus would sing this ancient prayer through me in order to lift my vibration. *O ma ha ne a, o tu tu ta te o*, which means: *o my God, I love you.* Sing the prayer and feel your energies come alive in you.

Now, move to your third chakra in the solar plexus area. Breath in and sound out the U. Feel the vibrations as they move through you bringing unification with your own Christ source. You may also say *I unite with the Christ within me.* Then sound out the U and experience the sensations in your third chakra.

Last, bring your attention to the heart chakra. Sound out the M. Feel the vibration in your heart center bringing mastery to the love within so it can be freely expressed. Remain in the heart and reverently say the prayer: *My God, my love,* three times. Now sound the M three times and notice what you are experiencing in your heart.

Chapter 14

The Spoken Word

In Shakti Yoga, we speak our prayers out loud with deep-felt sincerity, speaking from the well of emotions that is within. When you speak with deep-felt emotion, your Spirit will begin to become alive within you. Your emotional body is the connecting link to your spiritual body.

Jesus Speaks on the Power of the Spoken Word

Thought is the creative vibration of life. As you speak, embrace the thought with your emotions and bring forth your desire into the word so that the word has the energy and vibration of truth, of spirit. The moment you bring the Spirit into the spoken word, the faster it shall manifest.

It is the energy in the word that gives power to the word. So as one speaks. so must he become the spoken word. Become the word of God by embracing the word until every atom of your being vibrates with the energy of the word. Then you are the living word of God. You are then in the state of love.

You will find that when the word is filled with the emotion of love, you can move into the all loving substance of God and you can manifest all things from the substance through your divine thoughts. When this concept is realized and understood, you serve the God of your being and your service is joyful.

You are King in your Kingdom and you will begin to experience having dominion over your life. You will then be living God's will for you and you then experience heaven.

Throughout your Shakti Yoga practice, you are using these principles. You will learn and understand the awe, wonder and power of the spoken word. You will begin to feel yourself become the substance of God. You will feel pleasure, light and timeless and you will know that all things are possible with God.

The Awe and Wonder of Becoming the Spoken Word

In 1994, I was leading a workshop to activate the sacred seals for a Michigan group. We had rented a retreat house in the country on a lake. (This work is best suited to a pure atmosphere in nature.) While laying on the floor with my arms outstretched from the shoulders, palms facing up, I was lost in God's love. **I had become one with the substance of God and was saying the attunement or prayer for activation.** When I was complete and had come back to this dimension, **I saw that there were cracks in the palms of my hands, just as if they had been sliced with a very fine razor. There was a cross design in each hand that was bleeding.** The bleeding lasted about four hours. Today, there are still crosses where my palms bled. **I was told that a stigmata had occurred in my palms while in this state of oneness with the divine.**

Chapter 15

Attunements Or Prayers

With each posture, we say a prayer. These prayers are designed to invoke the divine within. They must be filled with your life essence and a moving power to bring forth your desired result. The prayers are directly and energetically linked to the chakra and energy system of the body. Jesus shared the spiritual wisdom of prayers with me in the four teachings that follow.

First Teaching From Jesus

When you hold the truth in your consciousness, you become the living word of God. You will then learn that Spirit is the fulfillment of the need. In speaking the prayers in Shakti Yoga, you become completely focused in the moment and devoted in movement and prayer. You have given God your complete being. Then, as you fully and completely give yourself to God, you become the vibration of the words that you are speaking. Once you have become the vibration of the words, they become alive with God's life and they will manifest.

Second Teaching From Jesus

When you hold the vibration of God in your being, you build your inner world as you choose. God is the fullness of all good. You will learn that when you are in need, you are feeling a sense of lack or emptiness. Bring your need to the God within and become filled with energy, love, wisdom or whatever is needed.

So, once again, while moving into the ancient postures and speaking the prayers aloud, focusing on and feeling from deep in your heart and soul what you are saying, you become the vibration of God. Your outer world is a reflection of your inner life, for in that moment of devotion, you are consciously choosing to be dedicated to your God. In turn, God fills your world with good.

Third Teaching From Jesus

You will begin to understand the spiritual truth of your prayers. Then, you will begin to feel the atmosphere of the light of God around you and within you. You will also begin to understand and feel that the Father and you are one. As you practice Shakti Yoga, your vibrations will continue to quicken and you will move into states of ecstasy and bliss. Your body and the atmosphere around it will be filled with light. You will feel as if you are in another state of consciousness bathed in beautiful energy. It is the Father within (God) consuming you.

Fourth Teaching From Jesus

As you express the words, let love flow through you. When love flows through your consciousness, your cells respond and are caressed by it. The flesh becomes radiant, renewed, purified and quickened in its vibrations. The I AM is expressed through the flesh, the mind becomes enlightened, and the soul becomes educated. The body becomes obedient to the Spirit and expresses Spirit through it. Putting into words my experience of what this feels like to have God caress you with love is very difficult. Being pleasured and bathed with God's love is beyond any human experience I ever had. Also, this is not a one time experience. It occurs each time that I allow love to flow through my consciousness and my physical cell body responds. Then, I feel intoxicated with love, lost in love as it consumes every cell in my body, bringing pleasure to the body, soothing the heart and emotions. I am suspended in a timeless love that is so complete that I cannot think of anything that I want or need. In that moment, I have everything.

The Prayer of Shakti Yoga

Beloved Father,
I devote this practice this day
to the evolution of my soul,
to the fulfillment of my destiny in service to the One,
and I allow myself to be purified
as I rejoice in the Kingdom of Heaven
and in the Love of God.
I give thanks for this blessing,
for these moments that I share with my body
and my Spirit in onement.
And so it is. Amen

Chapter 16

Service To the God Within

Jesus would give me one lesson daily. Some lessons would be repeated for several days or even months until I understood for myself what they meant and how I could use this wisdom to realize my oneness with the Father-Mother God within.

Jesus Teaching on Service

It is your willingness to serve God that opens the doorway within to the Kingdom of God's Wealth.

These were beautiful words, but what did they mean in my everyday life. I learned to listen to myself and observe my thoughts about this concept of serving God. Just the word service triggered a negative response in my mind and body. I will share how I overcame this negative response and fully and joyfully embraced service.

EXERCISE—Read the concept: *It is your willingness to serve God that opens the doorway within to the Kingdom of God's Wealth*. Now, close your eyes and notice how your body responds to this concept of service. What does your mind chatter say? Watch your thoughts as if you are viewing a TV screen. Become an observer of your mind chatter.

Write how your body responded to the concept of service.

_____

_____

What thoughts came to you about this concept?

_____

_____

_____

_____

What were your feelings about service to God?

_____

_____

If you found any doubt, confusion or resistance to living in service to God, then **talk out loud** to this part of yourself. Give yourself guidance and encouragement as if you were speaking to a friend or your inner child. This may take more than one conversation depending on how much resistance there is. Once this resistant aspect of you chooses to join you in your service to God, you will find that you feel more congruent within yourself. You will move at a much more rapid pace into alignment to God's will for you. This occurs because your soul has begun to return home to the Father's house and its original purpose.

Each day, as you continue to ask for your service, you will find that good begins to bless your life. Life becomes effortless and you feel your oneness with the God within. The Father within becomes your partner in life. You are no longer alone, but now you are supported in life by the divine source within.

A Second Truth on Service

The servant seeks to attain and live outside of the Father's house.

We can attain all things by looking within ourselves and living in the Kingdom, in the Father-Mother God's house. We live outside of the Father's house when we think we are doing it alone. The ego is trying to make it all happen and then we come from need. The need may be to achieve material possessions, to feel important or to be acknowledged by others. When we come from need, we are projecting ourselves into life. Jesus would tell me: ***There is no need to project yourself. Know that you are the truth of God. You are not here to be receiving applause or to be greater than another. You are here to serve the Father within you.*** This always brought me back into alignment. Then, I could surrender my need to be receiving from outside of me. I could once again bring my focus back to my service to God in that moment.

This takes conscious commitment and practice. So, be patient with yourself. You are learning a new way of living and the ego personality self is dissolving. The old behavior patterns begin to break up and dissipate. Your addictions will begin to fall away one by one. All this is done in service to the God within.

As you continue to ask God for your service, you will begin to receive divine messages of truth. Through this process, you will find that you move very rapidly through the darkness, cleansing and purifying your mind, body and soul, because you are working at the atomic level of your being, recreating your cells to radiate and vibrate the truth. The body is becoming clearer; a clearer channel for the God of your being.

We begin our Shakti Yoga by asking the God within for our service. In this way, we begin to know God's will for us. Jesus would say to me, **God knows and man thinks (the ego)**. In my experience, service is always to evolve or develop myself. It may simply be to give myself what I need, to know something, to acknowledge that I am loved or to be kind to myself. They may be expressed like this; *Rest to remain in balance,* or *Know all is in divine order,* or *Accept that you are loved,* or *Keep walking forward on your path.* This practice puts me on my path of truth and purpose.

As you serve God, He in turn serves you even greater, is what Jesus taught me. This is the law of giving and receiving. You begin to know that the God within will serve you and this is a very secure feeling. Then, you are relying on God for your needs. God becomes your partner and greatest friend in life.

As you practice living in service to God, your wants will greatly diminish because you are being filled with such love. This leaves you feeling lighter, freer, more complete and safe.

A Message From Jesus On Service

There is but one choice, one purpose, one truth, and one science. First, you must choose God. Then have it be your purpose to serve God. As you serve God, He in turn serves you even greater. Then you become God. As you become as God is, you then can express God's goodness and grace through you. Man is the Christ of God, the ideal of God, created in God's image and likeness. You must have the intention to be and live the truth of God, for in this way you live the true Science of Life. You will become God's ideal man, God's ideal woman; a Christ. Rejoice in this journey home to the Beloved Father within you.

Choosing God

There is but one choice, one purpose, one truth, and one science. First, you must choose God. Then have it be your purpose to serve God.

When I began to look at these powerful statements and realize what they meant, I was overwhelmed with the changes I would have to make in my life to fulfill this and live the true science of life. I wasn't sure that I was ready to surrender so much of my ego to God. So little by little, I began to surrender my old ways of life. As I became more comfortable with this process of surrendering my ego, I began to feel the truth of who I am inside me, no longer so fearful and selfconscious. Then, I couldn't wait to choose God in other areas of my life. I decided to choose God instead of choosing to get attention from outside of me. I asked God for help in prayer.

My Prayer

Beloved Father, I love you and I need you to help me
overcome my need for attention from the world around me
I'm tired of trying to please the world.
I truly desire to live for you and please you, my beloved Father.

Once I made the choice to live for God, I became very conscious of how I wanted and needed attention from others. Here is an example of how I began to notice different aspects of my personality.

In classes at my health club, I would be totally absorbed in my own yoga practice. I do yoga with my eyes closed which takes me into bliss. When I opened my eyes, I became aware of my thoughts of being judged or fearing the judgement of others in the class. I was different because I had all of this blissful energy moving through my body. Many of the others were new to yoga and came for the exercise. They were not on a spiritual path and certainly not aware of the divine energy within them. Ten or fifteen minutes later, there would be a different aspect of myself that I would notice: a part of me that felt proud that she was so spiritually advanced. As you can see, I was trapped in fear and pride; part of me feeling fearful of being judged because I was different and another aspect of me feeling proud of my perceived advanced spiritually.

Each time one of these unhealed, unenlightened aspects of me would raise her head, I would ask her to come home and choose God. I would tell her that God is the source of her good and that she could and would receive what she needed from the God within. This process of lovingly teaching and guiding my unhealed part of self continued for about one month. I was teaching myself a new truth and also developing discipline as I guided myself back from the outside to the God within. One day, I felt something new inside. These aspects of self were receiving from within. I felt filled and complete with no desire to receive attention from the world around me. I no longer cared what the world thought of me. I was free. My posture changed, my shoulders opened and I could carry myself with love and certainty for I was living the truth and serving God, not those around me.

AS I SERVE GOD, I SERVE MYSELF
(MARCH 1999 REALIZATION)

This work is continually unfolding within me. That is what makes my life and this work so exciting. As I use these simple truths, I continue to grow, expand, purify and ascend to the next level of understanding and truth. I just recently realized that- as I serve God, I am serving myself. This morning, I woke up feeling extremely tired. I have been battling a low grade infection with aches, fevers and a sore throat. The symptoms come and go. This morning, I just wanted to sleep. The phone woke me at 8 am, a time when I'm usually up and active, but I wanted to roll over and go back to sleep. I had planned to go to my health club and participate in a body building class and then swim and work on this book. I've trained myself to speak to God as soon as I'm conscious and I asked God, *How may I serve you today? Is it in service for me to rest in bed or to go to the club?* The answer came: *Go to the club. You will find joy and inspiration there.* I then pulled myself out of bed and off I went. The class was just what my body wanted, even though my body was still tired and aching. Then, at the pool I rested in the sun for a half an hour before going into the pool. As I jumped into the pool, I felt my entire being shift and joy began to fill every cell until I felt effervescent in my entire being. I swam and played until I was complete. When I went back to my lounge, there were no aches or symptoms left in my body. Then, as I began to work on the book, I immediately was filled with creativity and inspiration. A plan for my work unfolded with each detail just spilling out of me. I was so high on life that I could hardly contain my joy. As I started to review this chapter on service and my little girl (ego) or unhealed self who was hanging out in fear said: *As I serve God, I serve myself.* All the fear was gone and joy and exultation filled my being. The vibration of my entire body had raised above the frequency of my aches, sore throat and fever and I was healed in the moment. I realized the truth through my experience of following my service for the day. This was an experience of physical, mental and emotional healing. God wants my highest good for me. On the other hand, my ego or unhealed self is always trying to figure out what to do and how to do it. Usually, it comes up with negative thoughts. By following my service, I moved right through my ego to my divine self which is filled with wisdom and creativity. Now I know exactly what to do and how to do it. My next step is to take action and follow through with my plan.

EXERCISE—Take a moment to go inside and see where you are ready to choose God. Maybe it is in relationships, maybe in your health or diet or your job. It can be in any area of your life. Jesus says, ***You must have the intention to be and live the truth of God. For in this way, you live the true science of life.***

Once you find one part of you that is ready to change, to choose God and have it be his/her purpose to serve God, say a prayer of intention. Write a clear and concise prayer and then speak it out loud into the universe. In this way, you gather the forces of the universe to support your intention and so it shall be.

_____

_____

_____

As you begin to look inside and observe yourself, you may become more conscious of your patterns, addictions and old ways of living. Don't make yourself wrong for this. Have this unhealed self choose God in the moment you notice the behaviors or hear the limited thoughts. You must be consistent and committed in order to heal. This is a very intentional practice working with the unhealed self. With continued practice, one day you will be free and living the truth of God. I celebrate your life and freedom with you.

Meditation In Preparation For Service

EXERCISE—We meditate to open ourselves to receive this divine service. Sit in Indian style or half lotus with your hands on your knees, palms open and facing upward. Imagine that you have a magic wand in your right hand. Raise your right hand in front of your face. Begin to sweep your auric field bringing the wand around and downward to the right knee and then over to the left knee and finally back upward to your head. This cuts the cords which are attaching you to others. As you make this sweeping movement, say this prayer:

Prayer

I clear my energy field
of anyone standing within it.
I bless them and send them to the light.

NOW, PLACE YOUR RIGHT HAND ON YOUR THIRD CHAKRA,
AND LISTEN TO THE GOD WITHIN YOU. Then say:

Beloved God,
how may I serve you?

As you quietly await a response, information may come to you in a sense of knowing. You may hear a voice, or a thought may be presented in your mind. This information is brief and to the point. Be patient and remain open to the possibility that your God knows and you will receive the correct information. You may choose to write your service down on paper or in a notebook. Frequently, when I receive information from my God, it is clear and vivid in the moment and then begins to fade within a few minutes, much like a dream, and I can't recall the details. So, I have learned the value of writing my service.

_____

_____

_____

Then, you must **trust this information and be willing to act on it, putting it into motion in your world.** This is the way to mastering yourself and changing your life experiences and circumstances. You will find that your desire to serve God will continue to expand and you will have a greater purpose to live life. Jesus would tell me: ***When you are serving God, your soul releases power and love into life.***

Chapter 17

Intentions and How to Use Them

The second step in Shakti Yoga is to take your service and make it your intention. Whatever information that you received while asking for your service from the God within is made into a statement of intention. It may simply be one word. Let's say your service was to *forgive*. You would stand and make a statement: *It is my intention to forgive*. When you stand and speak your intention, you are making a commitment to yourself and the God within. You are living in alignment to your highest good. **It is through your thoughts, deeds and actions that you live in alignment to God's will for you.** As you speak your intentions, you begin the process of transforming your ego and compulsive behavior patterns.

Your ego will continue to dissolve its need for control as you begin to rely on God more and more. When you speak your intentions from your service, it sets change in motion. You begin to heal your mind, body, and emotions. Your energy field will begin to clear and you will become more as God is. The divinity within will begin to dissolve the old ways of thinking, acting and feeling as you take these high intentions into your Shakti Yoga practice.

The intentions of your thoughts can change your perceptions which will change your experience. Put forth your intentions to receive the truth. **When you put forth your intentions in the spoken word, they can**

change time, erase distance and affect all things both seen and unseen.

The purpose of speaking intentions is to become the living word of God and to manifest the word. As you speak your intention, the energy leaves your body transmitting it to the universe. You feel this in waves leaving you and you know in that moment, that it is done. Then, you have become the living word of God and the word shall manifest. As you continue to surrender the ego's old patterns, you become clearer, more powerful and you will manifest more quickly.

The process of speaking your intentions leads you into the third stage of Shakti Yoga, which is mastery. Mastery is the experience of manifesting your intention. You will have mastered your thoughts, your emotions and your body. Your body will then respond to your spirit. Jesus would tell me, *Let spirit have full sway in your body.* That is why you may experience spontaneous movements in the body as you practice the yoga. Your spirit is moving you. In that moment, body and soul become one force, and as one force, you manifest. You are one and no longer split into fragments.

I will share with you how I have taken my own intentions and raised them to the next level where I experience instant transformation. I allow the wounded part of myself (the fearful or resistant or ego self) to speak the intention. This is the part of me that needs to be healed. My ego is in that moment surrendering to God's will or divine plan and the fear or resistance is dissolved, my energy is heightened and I am a reborn being. My weakness becomes my strength and I am filled with love and power.

When you stand and speak your intentions, you may experience your body begin to vibrate or a breath may spontaneously move through you. You are raising your vibration, consciously choosing a new way, a new life, the life of God, union with the Divine. In this process of speaking intentions aloud, you are implanting this vibration into your soul and it shall manifest. **You are working with the Divine in partnership. The grace of God will be upon you. In my classes, when students sincerely speak their intentions from the heart and soul, the waves of energy leaving their bodies can be felt as tingles and shivers throughout the room.** This is a sign that their intention is on its way to manifestation.

Teachings from Jesus

True power is in the truth of God. Speak the words of truth and love and let yourself be filled with your own vibrations of love and light.

Intentions bring you into oneness with the Father within, for in this way you begin to live a life of focus, a life of goodness. You engage your Divine Spirit and you begin to allow this Divine power that is within you to live your life, letting go of the needs of the ego. You begin to live the truth of your Divine Self, which is love, grace and God power.

Your deeds, your actions become pure. Honor returns to you and then you are living your Christ Self. The life that you live becomes dedicated to the God within. You live a life of devotion to God by your deeds, actions and the thoughts that you hold. Your intention creates movement forward. You are consciously choosing to live in alignment to God's will for you.

Stand and speak your intentions into the universal river of consciousness. By having an intention and speaking it, you begin to focus on the truth, on love and this tames your animal soul. With your intentions, you take control of your life and you return home to the Beloved Father within you.

As you put forth your intentions, they will manifest for you. This manifestation will become swifter and swifter as your power grows.

I salute the Christ of your being, God's ideal woman, God's ideal man. Your brother in service, Jesus of Nazareth

The Angel Of Devotion

Chapter 18

The First Stage of Surrender

The first stage of surrender captivates your entire being, bringing all the chakras into alignment to God's life. This is the life of love and light that is within you. The postures in this series develop your relationship with the God within through devotional love. **You are developing a love that is based on trust.** This stage of surrender is reached through devotion to the Mother-Father God within. Deep in the soul is the desire to love God. It is the forgotten song we wish to sing.

A Teaching From Jesus On Devotion

Whatever you are devoted to, you become. Devote yourself to the almighty, indwelling God, the love and the truth that you are.

Shakti Yoga leads you into a deep state of devotion to the God within. You will learn to focus your mind on devotional prayers. As you focus on the prayer (the thought), you are learning to master your mind by stilling the chatter. In this way, you are learning to control your thoughts and not be at the affect of the undisciplined mind. Then, you will be feeling your love for God as you speak the prayer aloud. This energy of love begins to multiply within your body which feels light, alive, tingly and vital. You may even begin to feel orgasmic pleasure as you surrender to God's love for you. Your body will be in devotion through ancient movements and mystical sounds. In this way, your entire being is in devotion: mind, emotions and body. As you deeply surrender to the energy of God, you begin to allow God to have full sway in your body. Then, you begin to become as God is. Jesus would tell me: **Whatever you focus on multiplies.**

By loving and blessing the Father within, you become the God that is within you.

Wisdom From Jesus

Your body must become obedient to Spirit to express God through it.

Your ego must yield to the pleasure of God moving through your body. As you devote your entire being to loving God, you are entering the state of surrender. The God within begins to expand and the energy of your own divinity begins to multiply. Your body becomes obedient to Spirit as the sacred energy moves through it, bringing it into the natural movements of surrender where your head begins to move back and your chest moves upward creating an arch in your spine behind the heart chakra. It may feel as though you are pinned back by the energy and unable to move. Do not be frightened, but allow these movements without controlling them. The God within will be moving and living through you. **You then have begun to manifest oneness with God in the physical form. To enter this state of oneness, you must have surrendered to your sacred energy (the God within). This is the natural evolution of your divine being coming to life, the life within.**

The key to developing a body that is obedient to Spirit is devotion. Jesus would tell me, *Your devotion to God must be all encompassing. You must live the life of truth, the life of devotion to God and not to the material world. Then and only then are you the heir to your Father's Kingdom.* You attain your experience of oneness as you deeply feel your love of God. When you speak your attunements (prayers), **feel each word**. Feel your love, then you are in the process of becoming the Living Word of God. This is the process of attuning yourself to the vibration of the words of love that you are speaking. As you do so, you are becoming the vibration of the words.

The Power of Devotion

Jesus explained the power of devotion to me in October 1998 in this way. When you praise, bless and worship the God within, you bring forth the power and love of God. Then, this power and love of God emanates from within you. The vibrations of God flow through you and around you. You envelop all with the vibrations of God.

Through your devotion to God, you become the vibration of God, the light of God. ***Then and only then do you have the power to conduct the forces of the universe***. You have become one with the light of God and the forces of the universe. There is no difference between you and God. You have become the same. You have become a spiritual being, not a material being, therefore, you have the power to conduct and direct the light of God outside of you as well as within you. For, in that moment, you are one with the light. If you love God with all of your being, it soon becomes a habit: it is your daily life and existence. You then have brought forth your divinity. As long as you stay true to the vibrations of God, you will never know strife nor will you perish.

When you unite with the God within, you can conquer all things. The power is drawn to you and generated within your body and it is sent forth to accomplish whatever you direct it to bring forth. This is God living through you emanating the force of good through you. When you send the Father before you to prepare your way, you are with God and the Father penetrates all things. Together you conquer that which is godly, godlike, good. You and the God within have become one force sent forth to manifest.

In my early years with Jesus, I was in such disbelief. This all sounded so easy. With Jesus coaching me, I learned how to send the Father before me. Each morning, prior to getting out of bed, he would have me send the Father before me to accomplish whatever I needed. To my surprise, it worked! Each time as I expand and manifest all that I need, then I move to the next state in my own development and again, there is the unknown with its challenges. I am asked to do things I've never done before and I face my own doubts, fears and unworthiness once again. I am still dissolving my walls of fear and doubt.

When I was living on the Big Island of Hawaii, Jesus suggested that I make a video of Shakti Yoga. Instantly I replied, *I'd love to, but where am I going to get the thousands for this project?* Jesus instructed me to send the Father before me, which I did. Amazingly enough, one evening I was teaching my weekly yoga class in the small town of Hawi, the most northern point on the island, and a man with a video camera entered asking if he could video our Shakti Yoga class for a community program to advertise the Hawi spiritual and cultural events. We were doing the yoga by candle light and I did not feel that it was appropriate to be filmed. However, I invited the man (David) to join us for the class, which he did. A few days later, we met for lunch and he agreed to film and produce my Shakti Yoga video. When I asked him the cost, his answer was heavenly. David said that it would be his gift to me in support of my work. The Father (God) had responded once again.

I invite you to send the Father before you in your life.
Here is the prayer Jesus taught me.
Beloved Father, go before me and prepare the way...
Then state specifically what you need.

The benefits of the first stage of surrender are so incredible. The greatest is entering into oneness with the God within you. This is the love that we have all been waiting for. As you develop this state of oneness, God will begin to think your thoughts and speak profound truth and wisdom through you as you. In this state of love, hormones are released from the pituitary and pineal glands. You will feel younger and excited to be alive. As you create this union with the divine God within, you are developing the power to manifest. God will respond to your desires and your requests. Jesus states it this way, *When you give your life to the Father-Mother God within, the source of your true love, wisdom and power, you enter the unknown state of oneness.* ***You must surrender to God to know God.*** *Once you have reached the state of surrendering to God, the divine energy of God will move through you as you.*

As you continue with your practice of Shakti Yoga and truly begin to surrender, you will begin to experience the presence of God within. This will allow you to surrender even more. You are coming to know God through your experience of His/Her Presence within. You will feel this Presence within you and all around you as love and as pleasure. It is as if you are intoxicated by God. This Shakti or Holy Spirit energy will be moving through your body and healing it.

As you deeply surrender, you will find that you loose interest in the material world. Jesus told me that: ***When you surrender completely to God, you live in the world, but not of it. You will not be involved in worldly activities, but only those that the Father-Mother guides you to participate in.*** Old patterns and needs will fall away. Even your addictions will begin to dissolve one by one naturally with no effort on your part.

When I began this journey with Shakti Yoga and Jesus, I was addicted to cigarettes. I had been smoking since I was a teenager. Slowly, I began to smoke less and less until one day I knew that I would never smoke again. This process took two years. I was not trying to quit smoking. It simply occurred as I began to hold more light in my physical body. The cigarettes were not of the same frequency that I was. So my desire was gone. I desired to feed my body food and substances of lighter frequencies.

The Divine Flow of Prayers in the First Series of Surrender

There is a divine flow to the prayers in the first series of surrender postures. The flow of postures, prayers and mystical tones creates a movement of your divine energy in your chakra system.

First, we begin to speak prayers of love and devotion to the Father-Mother God within. **These devotional prayers bring us into a state of oneness with God**.

Second, the flow of prayers moves to the next octave. **This is giving your life to God**. You will no longer be separate from God because you begin to feel the life of God within you.

Third, as you continue the prayers, your vibration quickens. Then, you move into **trusting God with your life. As you trust, God will begin to heal the betrayals, disappointments, abandonments and rejections of your life and relationships. Your vibration will quicken even more and you begin to purify at a cellular level.**

First Series of Surrender Postures

The right side of the body is our male energy, also known as positive (electrical) energy. The left side is our female energy, also know as negative (magnetic) energy. In some cultures, the male-female energy is referred to as Yang and Yin. In Shakti Yoga, we refer to the male side as The Beloved Father and female side as The Beloved Mother. The Father energy is the Light of God, holding our wisdom, guidance, strength, courage and protection. The Mother energy is the Love of God, holding our compassion, intuition, gentleness, kindness and nurturing qualities.

Always begin the leg postures with the right leg as this works in harmony with the natural flow of energy in the physical body. Working in opposition to the energy in the ascending colon may create a blockage.

Lie down on your back with your legs fully extended, your arms at you sides and the palms of your hands facing upwards. Relax. Take a moment to let the body blend right into the mat, consciously letting go. Breathe deeply into your body and sound out the ancient sound of AUM, letting go of any old thoughts, concerns, worries and doubts that you have brought with you.

Bring your right knee to your chest, embracing it with your arms and pulling it as close to your body as you can on the outbreath. Keep your shoulders relaxed (Fig. 1). In this way you open the first chakra, preparing to surrender into the divinity within.

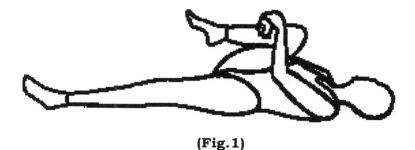

(Fig. 1)

Take a moment and feel your love for the Father within. Let this love for God fill you. Become completely focused and devoted to your love for the Father. Nothing else exists in this moment but your love for God. Speak the prayer aloud and sound out the AUM. (The pattern of speaking a prayer and sounding the AUM continues in each posture.)

PRAYER

Beloved Father, I love you.
I love you with all of my heart, with all of my mind
and with all of my strength.

Aum

Breathe in and as you exhale, bring your knee even closer into your body surrendering a bit more into the posture and once again, sound out the Aum.

Place your left hand on your right foot, gently guiding the foot over to the left thigh, then let the right knee fall to the floor. Allow the weight of your knee to take it toward the floor. Bring your right arm above your head extending it fully and elongating the right side of your body. (Fig. 2)

(Fig. 2)

PRAYER

I willingly surrender.
I surrender to the will of God for me,
and I allow myself to move forward in truth
and in love serving you.

Aum

Surrender as you open your hip joint and pelvic area, opening the first and second chakras. Feel your willingness to serve God and your willingness to surrender. Let yourself open to this concept. Let your body open to the energy of surrender and service.

Bring your right hand down and grasp your right foot. Bend the knee and pull up on the foot keeping the sole of your foot parallel to the opposite wall. Your knee will gently move closer to your head. Bring your left arm above your head, point your left toes and stretch with your left arm and hand. (Fig. 3)

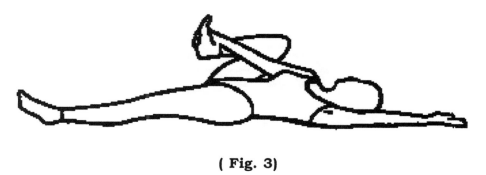

(Fig. 3)

PRAYER

I am your child.
I come to you in pureness,
and in vulnerability,
and I open my heart to love you.
I open my mind to hear your wisdom.
I open my body to serve you.

Aum

Feel your vulnerability as you open and know you are safe in God's loving presence. Remember, the Father is within you and you are within the Father.

Raise the right foot to the heavens and then gently pull down with your right hand so that the knee moves closer and closer towards the earth, opening the hip and groin areas (Fig. 4),letting go.

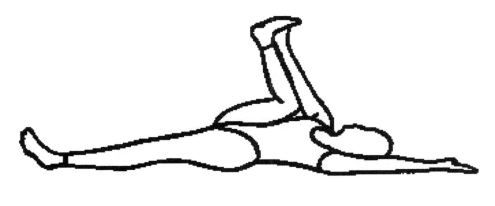

(Fig. 4)

PRAYER

Beloved Father,
I surrender to you.
Consume me with your love
and heal me.

Aum

Take a moment to feel the energy of the Father's love for you consuming you, healing you, and give thanks.

Let go of your foot, allowing your foot to begin to rise upward. Bring your arms straight out from your shoulders, palms facing up. Slowly, let your leg fall open and downward to the right. Roll your foot to the right as the inner thigh opens. (Fig. 5)

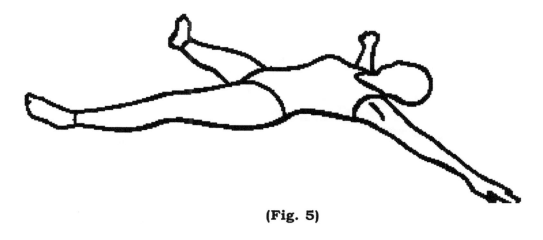

(Fig. 5)

PRAYER

Beloved Father, I give you my life.
Take me. I am yours.
Take me and make me whole.

Aum

Feel yourself yielding to the Father. Open your heart as you have never opened it before.

Turn your head to the right keeping your right shoulder on the mat. Let you right leg cross over the body, letting the weight of the leg open your spine as you twist, allowing the vertebras in your back to open. (Fig. 6) Let go and let God flow freely through you. Aum

Now arch your back, breathe into your heart chakra, keeping your right shoulder on the ground. Open to life, to joy and to love. (Fig. 6)

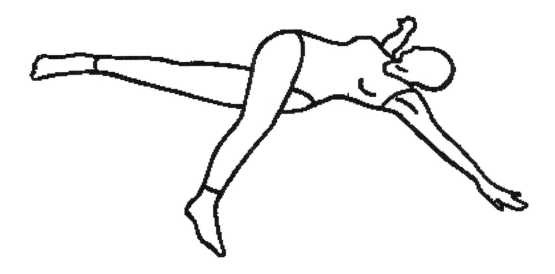

(Fig. 6)

PRAYER

I thank you Father. I love you Father
and I love myself. I thank myself
for allowing myself to be in this moment
surrendering and realizing the truth of my being.

Aum

Return your leg back to center and allow it to come back down on the mat. Bring your arms back down to your sides and feel the energy in the right side of your body.

As you continue to lie basking and bathing in God's love, say a prayer of thanksgiving.

PRAYER

Beloved God, I give thanks
for this moment of now,
for living in oneness with you,
serving you and living you through me.

Amen, Amen, Amen

Bring your left knee to your chest, embracing it with your arms and pulling it as close to the body as you can, keeping your shoulders relaxed. (Fig. 7) In this way you open the first chakra, preparing to surrender into the divinity within.

(Fig. 7)

PRAYER

Beloved Mother, I love you.
I thank you for your
nurturing love.

Aum

Feel the Mother's love for you. Accept that this love is renewing and restoring your body to its perfection.

Place your right hand on your left foot, gently guiding the foot over to the right thigh, letting the knee fall to the ground. Allow the weight of your knee to take it toward the mat. Bring your left arm above your head elongating the left side of your body. (Fig. 8)

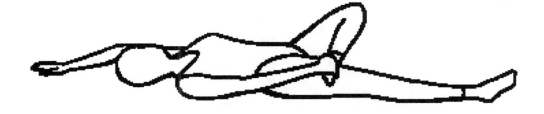

(Fig. 8)

PRAYER

I surrender to your kindness,
Beloved Mother.
I no longer resist you.
I let your love
come forth from within me.

Aum.

The Mother's love can heal your broken heart. She can heal the emotion of pain. Open yourself to receive her gift of loving kindness.

Bring your left hand down and grasp your left foot. Bend the left knee and pull up on the foot, keeping the sole of your foot parallel to the opposite wall. Your knee will gently move closer to your head. Bring your right arm above your head, pointing your right toes and stretching with your right arm and hand. (Fig. 9)

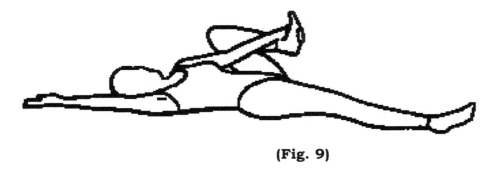

(Fig. 9)

PRAYER

Beloved Mother, I love you
and I need you.
I am your child
and I devote myself
to you in this moment.

Aum

Feel your devotion and love for the Mother within. Focus your mind on your love for her.

Raise the left foot to the heavens and then gently pull down with your left hand so that the knee moves closer and closer toward the mat, opening the hip and groin areas (Fig. 10), letting go.

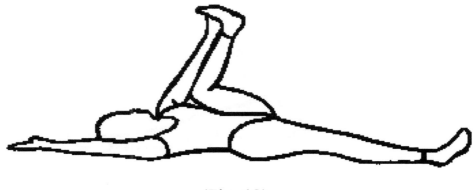

(Fig. 10)

PRAYER

I surrender my mind.
I surrender my heart.
I surrender my body to you,
Beloved Mother, and I love you
with all that I am in this moment.

Aum

Feel the love that is being offered to you in this moment. Allow yourself to receive more fully than you've ever received before. As you serve the Mother, she serves you even greater.

Let go of your foot, allowing your foot to begin to rise upward. Bring your arms straight out from your shoulders, palms facing up. Now let the leg fall open and downward to the left. Roll your foot to the left as the inner thigh opens. (Fig. 11) Feel vulnerable in this position and remember that you are safe in God's love.

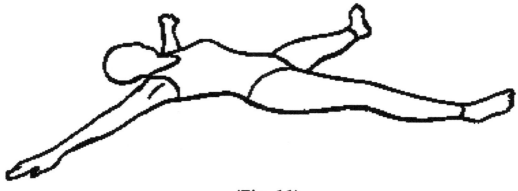

(Fig. 11)

PRAYER

I give my life to you
fully and completely Mother,
in this moment and forever.
I am here to serve you
and I love you now and forever.

Aum

As you give your life to the Mother, you become the life of the Mother. She will begin to love through you, as you.

Turn your head to the left, keeping your left shoulder on the mat. Let your left leg cross over the body, letting the weight of the leg open your spine as you twist, opening the vertebras in your back. (Fig. 12) Let go and let God flow freely through you. Aum

Now arch your back, breathe into your heart chakra and keep your left shoulder on the mat. Open to life, to joy and love.

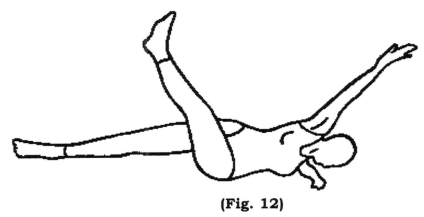

(Fig. 12)

PRAYER

I thank you Mother. I love you Mother
and I love myself. I thank myself
for allowing myself to be in this moment,
surrendering and realizing
the truth of my being.

Aum

Return your leg to center allowing it to come back down to the mat. Bring your arms back down to your sides and feel the energy in the left side of your body.

You will now be working with both legs: left, the Mother (Female Principle of Divinity) and right, the Father (Male Principle of Divinity). These postures are designed to open the lower back where the second chakra is located. This is the chakra of relationships and you will be developing your relationships with the Mother-Father God. The divinity of the second chakra is developed through trust and these prayers are designed to bring you into the state of trust.

Bend both knees, pulling them into the chest (Fig. 13), embracing them with love and gently pulling them even closer to your chest as you exhale.

(Fig. 13)

PRAYER

I trust you with my life
Beloved God.
I trust you.

Aum

Begin to become aware of your state of being. Are you resistant to trusting God with your life?

Place the soles of the feet together. Bring your hands inside your knees and take hold of your feet with your hands interlacing your fingers. Just allow your knees to fall open as you press the soles of your feet together. (Fig. 14) This creates a pyramid over the first chakra.

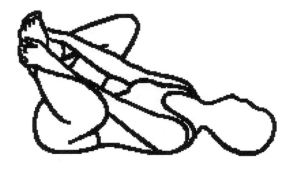

(Fig. 14)

PRAYER

Beloved God,
you are within me and I am
safe in your love and light.

Aum

Let yourself begin to sink into feeling safe with the God within.

Part your feet and hands but continue to grasp the feet with your hands. Pull up on the bottoms of your feet so that your knees move toward your shoulders. (Fig. 15)

(Fig. 15)

PRAYER

I trust you
Beloved Mother-Father God,
to bring me the love that I need to heal,
to grow and to be nourished
in this dimension.

Aum

Allow the energy of safety to fill you. Let the muscles relax in your back. Feel your spine softening as you let go.

Lift your feet toward the heavens. As you exhale, pull down on your feet, bending your knees and bringing them closer to the earth. (Fig. 16)

(Fig. 16)

PRAYER

I surrender now.
It is safe to surrender to you,
for I am safe in your love and light.
I trust you to lead me home.

Aum

This is the greatest opening in the lower back. Feel your second chakra opening as your trust is deepened.

Extend your arms out from your shoulders, palms facing down. Let your knees fall to the right as your head moves to the left. (Fig. 17) Keep your left shoulder on the mat.

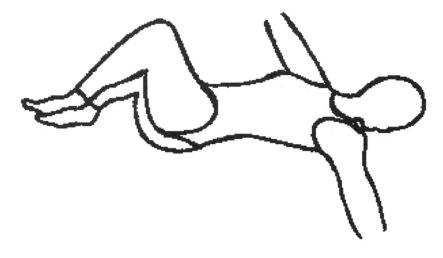

(Fig. 17)

PRAYER

I am teachable.
Teach me what I need to know.
I surrender to your wisdom.

Aum

Feel how relaxed your body is. Feel how peaceful you are as you surrender deeper and deeper into the God within.

Reverse sides now and move your knees to the left and your head to the right. Keep your right shoulder on the mat. (Fig. 18)

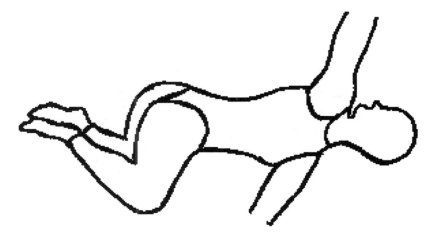

(Fig. 18)

PRAYER

I surrender to you. Lead me home.
Lead me, Beloved God of my Being,
and I shall follow you.
I am yours now and forever.
Teach me. I am teachable.

Aum

Return your legs back to center, extending them and resting them on your mat. Feel the beauty of God within each cell, blessing you and loving you.

Gently and tenderly, place your hands on your body wherever they are drawn. Let the healing energy flow through you.

As you continue to lie basking and bathing in God's love, say a prayer of thanksgiving.

PRAYER

Beloved God,
I give thanks for this moment of now
that I am in oneness with you,
serving you,
living you through me.
Amen,
Amen, and Amen.

The Angel Of Surrender

Chapter 19

The Science Of The Body
In Second Stage Surrender

THE SECOND STAGE OF SURRENDER IS A MOVEMENT OF THE PURIFICATION OF THE SOUL.

The soul is a recorder of your experiences. It records what you have embraced emotionally to be used as a reference. When you have an experience, your soul searches itself for a similar memory which may have been an experience of love, abandonment or betrayal. Your body remembers that it has felt this sensation before. You may find yourself reacting to the circumstances of your life from your soul memory. When we react, we are out of control and at the effect of life.

Jesus says that the Mind Of The Body holds the past. The Mind Of The Body is our human appetite for instant gratification and our need for possession. (the material plane).

HOW THE SOUL IS IMPRNTED

Thought is lowered into emotion. Emotion is then lowered into matter. Once the body feels the impulse of the sensation of emotion, it is recorded into the soul and memory is created. Therefore, what we choose to think and feel is very important because that is what we become cellularly.

During each session of Shakti Yoga that you participate in, you are engaging your mind, body, emotions and soul. You are becoming a higher vibration cellularly and your soul is becoming educated and purified.

The soul goes with you into each lifetime. The soul is you. It brings with you the wisdom you have gained along with the distorted consciousness (all that needs to heal) so that your soul can become educated and evolve.

You enter your soul when you begin to feel. Your passport into your spirit is emotion, deep-felt emotions of love and of pain. That is why you are asked in the first stage of surrender to continuously feel the prayers and to feel your love for God. Remember, deep in your soul are the songs of love we wish to sing to God. In the second stage of surrender, you are asked to surrender into your pain so that you can be purified.

The Second Stage Of Surrender

The second stage of surrender is a movement of the soul. It is an opportunity for a miracle. Jesus says, ***In the state of surrender, the possibility for all things is available***. In this stage of surrender, the cells are cleansed and they release the old structure of energy they have been holding, such as: sadness, suffering, separation, pain, fear, anger. Once this old structure dissipates, a new energy or new life can take its place.

This state of surrender is an experience of building your faith and trust in God, the source of your good. It is also an experience of your vulnerability, your courage and your strength. You are given the opportunity to surrender all that you are not. You are not your anger, your sadness, your illness, nor the circumstances in your life. **You are the truth of God, which is the goodness and grace of God's love and life.**

You can decide **what** and **how much** you wish to surrender. You may choose to surrender a little bit or all of yourself and your situation. Through this process of surrender, freedom awaits you.

In order to get to the other side of your blockage into the unknown state of freedom, you must be willing to be out of control in the moment of surrender. As the old consciousness is dissolved within, you will find your true God self. You will find that your truth and wisdom is within and always has been.

When you have a need, such as: the need to be loved, accepted or appreciated, then you will try to control others. Jesus says, ***When you surrender your needs, you let go of control. Then you become the almighty indwelling God. You are then free. Surrender the need to control. Your personality self is filled with the need to attain*** *material possessions. You are driven to be perfect, accepted, smart, loved, beautiful and successful. You try to control life to attain and fulfill these needs. It is an impossible task. You can only find true love and fulfillment through God. You are in control when you become One Force, One Focus, One with the Infinite Mind of God.*

This wisdom will serve you to free yourself from your attachments and your investment in having things a certain way. Now when you find yourself affected by other people's actions, immediately look inside to your need, then surrender it and you will be at peace once again.

The second stage of surrender is also a very vulnerable state because you truly begin to look inside yourself seeing your fears and needs. It takes courage to face your darkness, no longer running away from yourself and your good. Jesus says, **This is a vulnerable state, for in the moment of surrender you have given up control (the ego). YOU MUST BE OUT OF CONTROL TO GAIN TRUE CONTROL OF YOUR LIFE. This state of surrender, therefore is an act of courage and strength.**

The key to your development *is to be willing to surrender into your darkness.* Feel the pain that has been locked within you. This takes courage and a profound desire to heal and be free. In the moment of true surrender, you give it to God. Speaking aloud, give a voice to the darkness and the pain. **This is crucial to the process of surrender. Your unhealed self must speak the words of surrender.** Ask God to lift the darkness and pain from your heart, mind, body and soul. God will take you by the hand and lead you into a **new life**.

When you are surrendering, you may experience the energy moving your head back. The Shakti or Holy Spirit may be so powerful that your body may arch or spontaneously go into its own movement (posture). You may even find yourself bouncing inches off the mat. The Shakti or Holy Spirit is dissolving the old structure of energy within you. Then you will be open and receptive to the wisdom and the truth.

As you develop your relationship with the God within through devotion, the Father-Mother becomes alive within you and respond to your prayers to be cleansed of your old energy patterns.

The first series of Shakti movements (postures) and attunements set the stage for the transformational experience of this second series.

PREPARATION

This state of surrender is more than a word. It is an experience that must come from deep inside of your being. You must be ready to surrender your old ways by being willing to give them to God so that they may be lifted. Please take the time to reflect and meditate on the exercises that follow. They will help prepare you for surrender.

When I go inside of myself, I see a door. I am on one side in the darkness of my limited mind living an illusion of unworthiness. On the other side of the door is the light of my freedom and I hold the key that unlocks the door. The key is surrender. All I have to do is have the courage to surrender and walk through to the light.

Jesus would tell me: *I will show you the way home to the Beloved Father, but you my beloved one must do the unfolding. No one can do this for you. Each must do his/her own unfolding to enter into the Kingdom of God's Wealth. Feel your sadness, your fear and your anger so that they may be transformed into joy. Worship God by the life that you live. Focus on your unfoldment staying steadfast to the vision of GOD I AM, CHRIST I AM. Become the ideal of God, a Christ.*

EXERCISE: Close your eyes and be with this message from Jesus. After a moment, answer the questions that follow.

What does this message mean to you?

_____

_____

Do you allow yourself to feel your darkness?_____If yes, briefly describe a recent experience.

_____

_____

How are you worshipping God by the life that you live?

_____

_____

How do you stay focused on your own unfoldment?

_____

_____

Teaching from Jesus: *This (surrender) is a vulnerable state, for in the moment of surrender, you have given up control (the ego). YOU MUST BE OUT OF CONTROL TO GAIN TRUE CONTROL OF YOUR LIFE. This state of surrender, therefore, is an act of courage and strength.*

EXERCISE Take a moment to contemplate this truth. Be with it and let it resonate with your being. Look inside of yourself, asking the questions that follow. Then, write what you realize about yourself in relationship with this truth.

What part of you is ready to heal?

_____

_____

What need are you ready to surrender?

_____

_____

Are you willing to be out of control so that you can gain true control of this part of you?

_____

The Experience Of
Awakening The Spiritual Senses

(THE BENEFIT OF GOING INTO YOUR DARKNESS)

The deeper you go into the darkness, the greater your rewards will be. As you open yourself up to vulnerability, exposing your shame, guilt, sadness, hate and anger to the God within and surrendering them, they are dissolved by the light and the love of God. Transformation occurs at the cellular level and your soul is purified.

Then you begin to awaken the spiritual senses that are within you. You will become more as God is, knowing what you need to know, feeling the love of God caressing your cells, and hearing the words of love from the love and light within. The love will speak gentle, soft and loving words of truth to you and you will feel this energetically as love caressing you. The light speaks to you of the truth of God. Wisdom is brought to you and you experience this wisdom energetically in your cells.

God is revealing to you the truth and imprinting it into your cells. As the imprinting continues, **you are becoming this wisdom and love cellularly and it is alive and living in this dimension to be shared and to be experienced**. Jesus would tell me: *It is time now to surrender and move into the light of God where all that you desire exists.*

You must have trust that the unknown state of freedom will be there for you. And, you must be willing to surrender your suffering, pain or lack in order to experience this new life of freedom. You are your own jailer keeping yourself locked in your illusion of unworthiness. Remember, you have the key to freedom and it is surrender.

This movement of surrendering your darkness cannot be forced. Once you choose to begin the process of surrendering, you will unfold naturally. The darkness will begin to come to light piece by piece. This darkness must be ready to return home to the Father's house. Be patient with yourself and have faith that you are moving into the light and love of God's Kingdom. If you weren't moving, you wouldn't be hearing this wisdom.

EXERCISE: From deep inside you, write your own prayers of surrender. **THE WOUNDED SELF MUST SPEAK THE WORDS OF SURRENDER. LET YOUR EMOTIONS COME TO THE SURFACE, BEING IN THE STATE OF VULNERABILITY**. Use these KEYS to assist you.

Be Humble and Vulnerable
Be Willing
Have Courage
Call Upon Your Strength
Make the Choice
Trust God

Second Series Of Surrender Postures

We are working with the concept of self-judgment. Is your self-judge ready to be healed, to choose to love self? If so, then accept your critical self and surrender into this energy of self-judgment. Deeply feel this part of you, and when you're ready, let your self-judge surrender to God.

Lie on your back. Place your hands under your buttocks, palms down. (This is the natural state of surrender that your body will move into as you surrender and activate your Shakti). Now, let the energy take you up on your elbows. (Fig. 19) Arch your back, lifting the chest and rest the top of your head on the mat.

(Fig. 19)

PRAYER

Beloved Mother-Father God.
I willingly allow the structure of my critical self to dissipate.
I surrender my critical mind, my critical eye, my self-judgment
and my self-hate, so that I may love myself as I am.
Aum

While in a sitting position, bend your right leg at the knee and let your right foot come up on the outside of your right leg. Keep your left leg straight forward. Now, if you can, lie flat on your back and extend your arms above your head. (Fig. 20) You may also rest on your elbows, forearms and hands, if you are unable to lie down on your back. (See Fig. 22) for an alternate arm resting position.) If you have knee limitations, you may not be comfortable in this position. Remember, always work at your own level of comfort.

As you speak the words of surrender, feel them deeply within your soul. When you speak from memories of the painful past, you are cleansing and purifying your soul.

(Fig. 20)

PRAYER

Beloved Father-Mother God,
I surrender whatever blockage I hold within my being
that keeps me separate from love; your love
and the love of those around me. And so it is.

Aum

Come out of the posture and resume a sitting position. Bend your left leg at the knee and let your left foot come up on the outside of your left leg. Keep your right leg straight forward. Now, if you can, lie flat on your back and extend your arms above your head. (Fig. 21) You may also rest on you elbows, forearms and hands, if you are unable to lie down on your back. (See Fig. 22 for an alternate arm resting position.) Now, with your mind, **go into any part of yourself that holds back in love, either in freely giving or in freely receiving love. Let this part of you speak the prayer.**

(Fig. 21)

PRAYER

I open my heart to you Beloved God.
Cleanse me of this old fear. Heal me, heal me, heal me. I am yours.
I desire to know of love fully and completely.
Heal me so that I may live in the river of love with no fear, no hate,
no separation; only love, joy and abundance.
Hear my prayer Beloved Father-Mother God.
Hear my prayer. And so it is.

Aum

From a seated position, bend both knees and bring your feet to the outside of your legs. You may stay in this seated position and place your hands on the mat behind your buttocks, fingers pointing away from the body. If you are able, you may go back down onto your elbows and forearms. (Fig. 22)

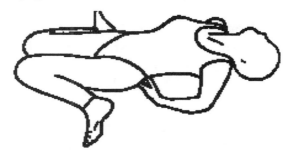

(Fig. 22)

For those who can, lie flat on you back and extend your arms above your head. (Fig. 23)

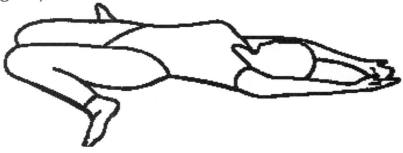

(Fig. 23)

PRAYER

Beloved Father-Mother God,
I surrender to you this fear of being loved completely,
and of loving completely.
Take this fear from my mind, my body, my heart and my soul,
so that I may serve you more fully.
Aum

The Law of Acceptance

We are now moving into the second stage of Shakti Yoga where we will be working with the Law of Acceptance. **Accept the truth for the truth shall set you free.**

Acceptance Begins The Healing Process

As you accept the truth, (be it the false truth you have held about yourself or the truth of God), your first chakra will begin to expand. The first chakra is the chakra of your life force energy, so you will instantly have more life energy flowing through your body.

When you accept a false truth about yourself, such as I am afraid I'll do something wrong, instantly you leave the state of denial. **When you live in the state of denial, you are truly dying. To enter the state of living and generating new life energy in the first chakra, all you need do is accept your feelings and limited beliefs about yourself and life.**

Once you truly become truthful with yourself and begin the process of accepting your darkness, this new life energy that you have created right within you moves up the central nervous system to the brain. The brain then begins to awaken from its dead sleep. **You then are free to accept the truth about yourself and a new energy will be sent throughout your system to every cell in your body. You are regenerating your physical, emotional and mental bodies with God's truth.**

Each time you move from the darkness of your own beliefs to accepting the truth, you string a pearl of wisdom on the silver thread of eternal life. When your silver thread is filled with your own jewels of wisdom, you will be illuminated. All of your blockages will have been dissolved by the light of truth, the light of God.

There are two phases of acceptance. The first deals with identifying and accepting the incorrect concepts, the false truths that you hold about yourself and life. The second phase deals with accepting the correct concepts, the new truth about yourself and life.

First Phase Of Acceptance

If at any time in the past, you have accepted that you are not good enough to receive or have what you truly wanted, then that energy is locked within you. This outdated energy keeps you from your dreams and the power to manifest them.

Our limited thoughts destroy us and cause us to age, to suffer, to live in pain. You die because you don't realize the truth.

If you are lacking in anything: love, money or health; look inside and examine the hidden concepts that you are emanating to the world that say you are not worthy or good enough. Begin to move into surrendering them to God.

The Concepts of Goodness or Badness

Often, as children, we were told that we were good, or the opposite, that we were bad, and believed it. Jesus says, *It is done unto you as you believe.* The world will treat you as if you are good, if you think you are good, giving you love, acceptance, and appreciation. The world is merely validating your truth. The reverse is also true. To the degree we have embraced that we are bad, we will be treated badly: ignored, criticized, not considered and so on. The world is saying: you think you are unworthy so I will treat you accordingly. Then we blame those that mistreat us and become their victims.

When we take responsibility for what we have conceived about ourselves, **we then have the power to change.** As soon as you accept the false truth you have conceived about yourself, it will begin to dissipate. When you become honest with yourself, seeing and feeling your pain, it frees you instantly. But, we hide from ourselves and pretend that everything is fine. We run away from ourselves by keeping busy, becoming workaholics or we cover our pain with sex, alcohol, drugs, sugar, shopping, caffeine, cigarettes, or any other addictive form that alters our pain. These are all forms of self abuse and self hate.

When Jesus was teaching me, he would stop me in one of these behaviors, interrupting me in the middle of my pattern, saying, *Face yourself. Once you face your false truth or fearful self, it will lose power over you.* He would tell me that this false truth, fearful self or self hatred was my devil or evil self and that I could dissolve it by just standing still and facing it head on. It took a tremendous amount of courage, but I did just that and found that it works. It is very scary in the beginning, but know that you're not alone. God is always with you to support you through your darkness into the light.

Jesus also explained that when I held an incorrect concept and truly believed it, that this was a false god I was putting before me. So when you begin to accept the truth, you are loving, honoring and worshipping God. Jesus says that, *You worship God by the life you live.*

When you take responsibility for what you have conceived about yourself, you then have the power to change, to be free from the incorrect concepts and false beliefs. You must first begin to empty out the old concepts and beliefs before you can begin to imprint the new concept.

Two Steps to Dissolving the Darkness
(false truths and incorrect concepts)

1. By accepting yourself exactly as you are, you are set free. If you are afraid, you must accept that you are afraid. Whatever it is, accept it and this starts the flow of energy that begins to dissolve the blockages. Say a prayer accepting your fear.

Beloved God, I accept that I'm afraid
there isn't enough for me and this isn't the truth.

Be specific and talk to God as if He/She was your dearest friend and truly loves and cares for you. Tell God everything, being honest, vulnerable and don't hold anything back.

2. Face the fearful self and surrender the fear and pain to God. Through surrender, the incorrect concept begins to be lifted and erased from your soul memory and then you are free to create whatever truth you choose. You can proceed with accepting the new truth, embracing the new truth and becoming this new truth. Here is an example of surrendering through prayer.

Beloved God, I surrender my fear that there isn't enough for me.
I give this to you. Take it. Take it from my body,
from my heart, from my soul and from my mind.
Thank you beloved God. I no longer need this fear
It is not the truth and I am ready to let it go and live the truth.

Second Phase of Acceptance

By accepting the truth of God, you will be quickening the vibrations of the body. Then, you will begin to vibrate the frequencies of truth. This cleanses your aura, stills your mind and purifies the soul. You will begin to embody the truth of God and this truth will be transmitted back to the Mind of God and the river of consciousness. These higher frequencies will assist in purifying the planet. When the truth of God is embodied within your flesh, you are living the truth for others to see. It is no longer only in higher realms of consciousness but available and living in the world. The truth of God will emanate from within you.

Jesus says, *Accept the thoughts of truth. Use your thoughts to build the mansion within of love, peace and harmony. As you accept the truth by experiencing the oneness, then the truth will become knowledge and it will be imprinted into your consciousness, your cells and your soul. Then, you will vibrate this wisdom forever. You will become the love of God. The Father within you will become you, expressing freely through you.*

Acceptance is the first step in manifestation. Change in your inner world will then be reflected in your outer world

Five Steps to Vibratory Transformation

1. Accept the truth, the new concept about yourself or life.

2. Embrace the truth, feeling the new concept. It is through feeling the new truth that it becomes you. It is recorded into the soul and imprinted into every cell of your human body. Whatever you become will be the experience that you will have in the outer world.

3. Know the truth, the new concept of self or life. Through the embracing process, the new concept becomes knowledge within you because it is you. You must feel something to know it. Then, you will know who you are.

4. Experience the truth, the new concept of self or life. You will have experiences to validate this truth or concept in your life because you are magnetically drawing a like vibration to you. The world is a reflection of who you are and what you feel and know about yourself.

5. Be the truth, the new concept. Being is the result of accepting and embracing a concept of truth. You are experiencing being the concept you have embraced.

The world is reflecting back to you your new concept. Then, you will experience a new life.

You Must Become What You Want To Manifest Or Experience In Life

You will find that the world will be different and you will be magnetizing to yourself new friends, new life and new experiences to mirror your new truth. This is the process of creating a new world. The power is within you to create whatever you need to fulfill your soul. I love sharing this with you because it works easily and rapidly. It is so exciting. All we need is the courage and strength to dive into the pain of the old concepts and surrender them to God.

This process of transformation in Shakti Yoga is very complete. In other forms of therapy, you empty out by feeling fear, rage, sadness or other feelings, but they don't transform completely. In the Shakti experience of transformation, you work with the Science of the Body and then you are working with God as your partner or therapist. God has the power to erase the old frequencies of thought that created the imbalance.

It is also essential to fill the void with a new imprint, a new vibration. That is why you accept the new truth, embracing it so that you can become the truth of God. Your soul is then educated and your body becomes obedient to spirit and you will be expressing the higher vibrations of God through you.

Wisdom from Jesus on Holding the Truth

When you hold the truth of yourself in consciousness, you can only experience yourself as divine. You can never change anything. You can rise above disease and disharmony to the spiritual truth, then the disease or disharmony begins to dissolve and change form. So, do not deny your fears; face them and move your consciousness to the spiritual plane; the one Mind of God where all truth is available and waiting to be accessed and lived. Man grows by realizing the truth of himself, expanding his consciousness, opening to the God within, to the truth that is waiting to be lived in each moment.

This wisdom from Jesus took me a long time to truly understand. *You can never change anything. You can rise above disease and disharmony to the spiritual truth, then the disease or disharmony begins to dissolve and change form.* Now I understand that my old concepts are my illusions and that I am experiencing in my life what I have embraced as the truth. It is my ego that embraced those concepts. The ego always wants to be right, control, manipulate and change through force. This doesn't work as I'm sure we all have experienced. Now, when I see my darkness or incorrect concept and accept it, then I can surrender it to God. As God lifts it, I can embrace the spiritual truth. That is how I can dissolve the disharmony or disease and rise above it to the truth. Then, I begin to experience a new life of harmony, ease, and joy.

Chapter 20

The I AM Principle

The I AM principle is a formula for changing the totality of your being, changing at the cellular level. In the I AM series of prayers and postures, we are working directly with the soul. **The soul records what we feel. As we embrace the prayers of truth that we are speaking, we are transforming ourselves from density into light.**

The key to the development of this series is to **feel the new concepts as you speak the words of wisdom and truth.** Feel and **embrace** your words as fully and completely as you can. **They must become you.** Bring the feelings from deep within your soul so that they may spring forth into life.

This series of postures brings balance and harmony to the male and female in each chakra. It creates a marriage, a union between the male and female energies in each cell of your body. A cellular renewal and reunion will also occur within each cell.

The **I** in the I AM is **male** and the **AM** in the I AM is **female. The purpose and the function of the female (AM), is to feel and embrace. The female becomes whatever she embraces. The female principle is creation. She creates by conceiving concepts and by feeling them.** When you hold a concept of life, or of self, and you embrace this concept, you are conceiving this concept into your total being, body and soul. Jesus says, *If man is to bring forth the Holy Spirit through him, he must embrace ALL THAT GOD IS.* This means that you must be willing to surrender the limited self-perceptions. The truth of God certainly isn't our deep, dark feelings of self. In healing myself and others for these eleven years, I have found that we don't like ourselves very much. We feel less than Godly and God like.

When we begin to allow the ego to transform into its true Godliness, **the ego must become humble and be pure in its desire to become as God is**. This is returning to our original state. **We already are all we could ever want to be, but we forget and put layer upon layer of false concepts over the true beauty of God that we each are.**

When the AM embraces that it is Godlike and Godly, then the I becomes these qualities that have been embraced and expresses them into life. The male (I) has the function of broadcasting the concept conceived to every cell of the body as a messenger of your perceptions of life. He then sends this frequency out into your energy field telling the world around what you have conceived. The world then responds to you according to your vibration. You magnetize to you a like vibration and you have an experience to validate your truth. This is the mirror process, which is that we are what we see in others.

EXAMPLE: If you embrace the concept, *I am love*, you begin to become the **identity of love and you begin to express love into life.**

God has many qualities and as you embrace each one, you become that quality and then you have a new identity. Your true identity becomes available to live through you and it is no longer distorted by the false perceptions of self.

If in the past, your identity was *I am less than Godly,* that is what you expressed through you. **This was the image of self you lived.** No wonder things didn't work out smoothly.

The I AM principle is an embodying experience. We have all held a tremendous amount of information in our intellect and we could spout it out and look great. There is a problem with this. It doesn't belong to us. We don't own it. It's just lip service because it hasn't become who we are. We then can't walk our talk.

As you embody the truth, the God within you expresses through you in the way you walk, talk and move through life *because that God truth is you.* The same is true when you have embodied a God quality, you feel the energy of the God quality moving through you. When you have embodied love, love moves through you and it feels delicious. If you have embodied power and certainty, you feel secure in yourself as these energies move through you. Feeling the God qualities that you have embodied moving in and through you is indescribably blissful.

When you begin to embody a new truth, you are becoming the electrical vibration of this new truth. The AM (the negative energy) embraces the new concept of God and that electrical frequency is sent from cell to cell by the I (the positive energy). As this is occurring, a quickening within the body is experienced as your vibration becomes faster and higher. Your limbs may even begin to move (kriya) uncontrollably. I see this as one cell tapping the cell next to it, broadcasting the good news from cell to cell throughout the entire body. A chain reaction begins to move throughout the cellular structure. If I was embracing love, the cells would begin to share the news: **I am love, I am love, I am love**, from cell to cell until my entire body was vibrating at the frequency of **love. Then, I would have become love in physical form. My Spirit, which is love, would be alive in each cell expressing freely into life through my eyes, smile, walk, talk and actions. That is bringing forth the Holy Spirit through you into life.**

The I is to realize and live that He is an individual expression of God. Then the I begins to feel His uniqueness and perfection, no longer striving to be like others and conforming. He no longer tries to be better than others because He knows that He is a perfect, pure and beautiful expression of God, living through a human body. He appreciates His gifts, realizing that there is no one exactly like Him.

The I AM Series Of Postures

Always begin on the left side with these arm postures. The left side is the feminine or the **AM** side of the body. From your lying down position, raise your left arm straight up to the heavens. Slowly, let the energy move your arm across your body to the right. Place your right hand between the shoulder and elbow joints and gently press downward to assist you in extending the stretch and opening the shoulder. (Fig. 24)

(Fig. 24)
Close your eyes and **embrace** the words of the prayer.

PRAYER

I am God's goodness.
I am God's grace.
God's goodness is within me.
God's grace moves through me.
I am God's goodness.
I am God's grace.

Aum

Release your left arm returning it to the mat. **Feel the energy of goodness and grace** that you are creating.

Raise your right arm straight up to the heavens. Slowly, let the energy move your arm across your body to the left as far as it will go. Place your hand between the shoulder and elbow joints and gently press downward to assist you in extending the stretch and opening the shoulder. (Fig. 25)

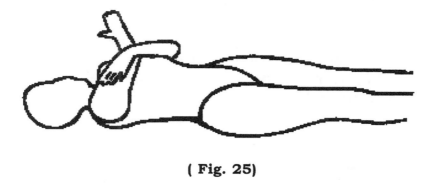

(Fig. 25)

PRAYER

I express into life
goodness and grace,
because
I am God's goodness
and grace.

Aum

Release your right arm and **feel the energy transmitting this truth into life.**

Place your left arm straight out from your shoulder, palm facing down. Bring your right hand over your left ear and guide your head to the right. (Fig. 26) Gently open and stretch the left side of your neck and shoulder.

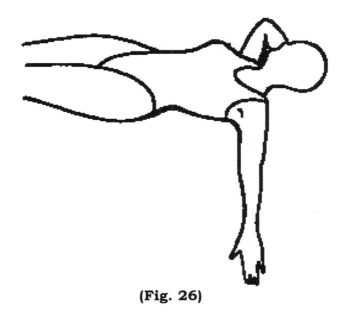

(Fig. 26)

As you embrace that the abundance of God's wealth is within you, God's abundance will become more available to you.

PRAYER

I choose to embrace abundance.
I am the abundance of God's wealth.
I choose to embody the abundance of God's wealth.

Aum

Release your right hand and let your head return to center. **Feel the energy that is moving all around you** (your electro-magnetic field).

Place your right arm straight out from your shoulder, palm facing down. Bring your left hand over your right ear and guide your head to the left. (Fig. 27) Gently open and stretch the right side of your neck and your right shoulder.

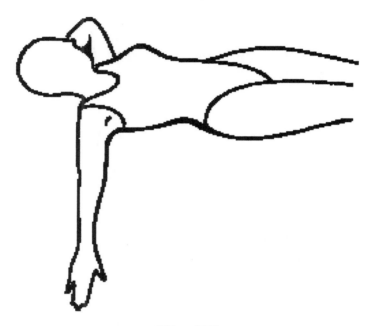

(Fig. 27)

The male (I) serves or brings to you whatever you have embraced. If you have embraced abundance, then this abundance is brought to you from all sources, both from within and also from the world around you.

PRAYER

I express the abundance of God's wealth through me,
for I am the abundance of God's wealth.

Aum

Release your left hand and let your head return to center. **Feel the atmosphere that is around you.** Your consciousness has been raised and your energy has quickened. You are transmitting a new frequency into the universe.

Chapter 21

The Temple

The Temple is a series of four postures: the Tabernacle, the Temple of Eternal Life, the Temple Flow, and the Mummy. These temple postures are very powerful and very pleasurable to your entire being. They are postures of energy, **pure divine energy.**

Without conscious thought, the energy will be moving your hands in an ancient flow that was taught in the mystery schools. You already know these movements as your soul remembers them. These movements take you into the DNA system of the body, the system of wisdom, knowledge and creation. Your body will create geometric symbols of movement throughout these postures.

You will be connecting the male-female energies and your body will begin a movement of giving and receiving from within. The energy flows between the male and female in a figure eight (the symbol of infinity). You may feel a rocking motion as you develop in these postures. Your rib cage will begin to move back and forth as the male and female energies intertwine and dance together. It is a very sensual, and yet, peaceful feeling. Your male-female energies come into balance. As you develop this energy within, your bones begin to float and align themselves.

You must surrender to the Intelligence of the Divine Energy and rely on it, allowing the Energy to have full sway in your body. Let it manifest within you. Give it permission to finally move in and through you. Any time your back is out of alignment or hurting, you can do this posture. Surrender to the Intelligence of your Divine Energy.

Jane, a student of Shakti Yoga shares her experience of doing the Temple flow. *I've been doing this posture for a while and I didn't have an explanation of this process. I have scoliosis and it has been helping tremendously. Things in my back begin to snap, move, break lose and correct. I found that I can move my hands over the different chakras and different parts of my spine move.*

The Tabernacle

The Tabernacle is created over the heart chakra. **Within the Tabernacle is the Chalice or Holy Grail that is filled with the Kingdom of God, God's Wealth, everything we could ever want or need**. Clairvoyants in my classes have described the Chalice as jeweled and incredibly beautiful.

In this posture, we take whatever we need or want and we drink freely from the Chalice, letting the Chalice fill us. If we find a lack or emptiness within us, we drink from the Chalice within, allowing it to fill every need, every lack in our lives. It's symbolic and it is also using our mind and our senses to experience being filled from within.

It is not only symbolic, but also energetic. **We become the energy of whatever we drink from the Chalice**. EXAMPLE: If we feel loneliness, we drink of love and companionship, and the energy of loneliness is dissolved and filled with love. Then, we will manifest companionship and love in our experiences in life.

The key to activating the flow of God's Wealth is to **realize that the Kingdom of God is within you. As you realize that and drink of your own Wealth, the Chalice begins to overflow with joy.**

The purpose of drinking from the Chalice is to be filled from within, to receive whatever you need in the moment from the Kingdom of God's Wealth within. As you practice this posture, you discover and begin to activate the divinity within you.

The Tabernacle Posture

Lie down, placing the soles of your feet together. Bring the palms of your hands together over your heart in a prayer posture. Allow yourself to feel the balancing within your body. Feel the peace of this positive-negative flow of energy as you give and receive within yourself. Let the energy move your hands up over your heart chakra, stopping half way up. (Fig. 28)

Enter the Tabernacle with your mind and senses. You find within you a beautiful Chalice. The Holy Grail is within you. In this Chalice lies everything you need. Rejoice in this knowledge. Everything is within your heart.

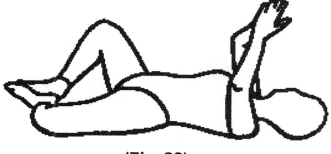

(Fig. 28)

Prayer

I drink of love.
I drink of perfect health.
I drink of peace and joy.
I drink of abundance.

Aum

Drink freely of everything you want and need. **Feel the energy filling you and freely flowing through you.**

PRAYER

I give myself what I have longed for
that I have never received from others.
I realize that everything
is within me and I am filled.
I give myself All That God Is
that I Am.
I am safe in my body.
and I am safe in my life,
for I Am As God Is
and there is nothing I need.

Aum

Lie in peace. Peace, be still. The body needs to be in peace to heal.

The Temple Of Eternal Life Posture

This posture signifies that the body is filled with the life of God. It is an opportunity to love you body, seeing it as God created it, perfect and divine. Once you begin to love your body, the body can begin to become the vibration of love. Healing can then occur instantly. You begin to regenerate new cells with the vibration of love and acceptance of self.

Let your hands move up over your head. This creates a pyramid over the crown of your head. Your legs remain in a pyramid form under the root chakra. (Fig. 29) The two double pyramids you are forming create a tremendous amount of power. Symbols are a way of creating energy and symbols also are a doorway into other dimensions and into the DNA.

(Fig. 29)

PRAYER

I love you body.
You are beautiful body.
You are the Life of God body, and I love you.

Aum

You may feel it appropriate to forgive yourself for expecting your body to be something God didn't create it to be, or for judging your body or expecting yourself to look a certain way.

PRAYER OF FORGIVENESS

I forgive myself for not accepting my body,
for not loving my body.
I forgive myself for judging my body,
and expecting it to be something
to please the consciousness of the material world.

Aum

Repeat a prayer of love for your body.

PRAYER

I love you body.
You are beautiful exactly as you are.
Body, you were created to express love
through your eyes, your voice,
your movements
and your touch.

Aum

The Temple Flow

The Temple flow is designed to acknowledge the light within the body. **This movement will create a divine flow of energy.** We repeat this movement three times.

The purpose of this movement is to dive into the darkness and bring light and wisdom to the unhealed self, bringing the divine energy into human form. There is a natural flow of energy that moves from the crown to the root chakra in a loop. When you are disconnected from the truth, this flow of energy is interrupted and you feel out of balance. We are reconnecting the divine flow within us.

This movement is a soul retrieval which frees you from your limited illusions of self and life. You are acknowledging yourself by anointing yourself. When you touch your lips, you are blessing yourself. Then, you bring this energy of anointing and blessing into the heart. From the heart, you turn your hands downward pointing toward the root chakra, where you dive into the lower aspects of consciousness and energy, your personality self, unhealed self or ego. Then, you bring your hands back from the root to the crown over your head, sounding the AUM. This dissolves the old, limited energy as it ascends from the lower chakras into the light.

This is a great act of love and compassion for self. You are finally beginning to love your darkness. Healing occurs when you have love and compassion for yourself.

THE FIRST FLOW

Let the hands move over the forehead. (Fig.30)

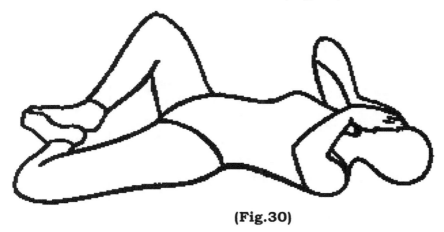

(Fig.30)

PRAYER

I anoint myself;
all that lives within my body.
I anoint my fears and my strengths.

Aum

Let the hands move down to your lips, kissing your thumbs as they
pass over the lips.

PRAYER

I bless all that I am.
I bless my fears and my strengths.

Aum

Now, let the energy move your hands to the heart center. (Fig. 31)

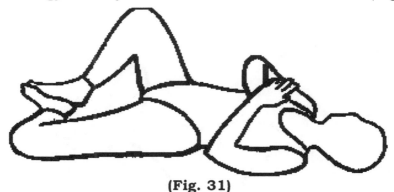

(Fig. 31)

Turn the hands downward and allow them to move down to the root chakra. (Fig. 32)

(Fig. 32)

PRAYER

I dive into my human self and I bring myself compassion,
understanding and love.
I bring tenderness to myself.
I praise myself for my willingness to be here,
to look at myself and be honest.
And I ascend my doubts now.

Aum

Bring your hands from the root to the crown. (Fig. 33)

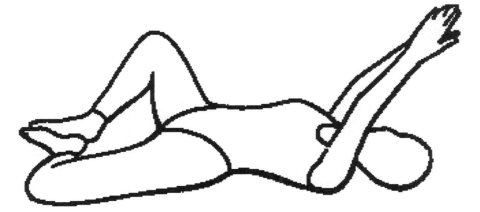

THE SECOND FLOW

Once again, allow the Grace of God to move your hands. Gently touch your forehead repeating the hand position of Fig. 30.

PRAYER

I anoint my fearful self.

Allow the Grace to move your hands down to your lips. As you pass over your lips, kiss your thumbs.

PRAYER

Blessed be I
who seeks the Truth of God.

Bring your hands down to the heart (Fig. 31),and point your hands downward, diving into your human self. (Fig. 32)

PRAYER

I dive into my unworthiness
and I tell my unworthy self.
You are worthy of God's Love,
God's Life and God's Kingdom.
I ascend my unworthiness.

Aum

Sound the Aum and return your hands from the root to the crown, above your head. (Fig. 33)

THE THIRD FLOW

You will be moving your hands from above your head (the crown) to the base of the spine (the root chakra) and then returning your hands back up to the crown to complete the third flow as in figures 30 through 33.

PRAYER

I anoint myself as God's perfect child,
perfect life, perfect creation.

I bless the life that I Am.
I bless my humanness.

I dive into my guilt.
I bless my guilt and return it
to God's Light and Love
to be dissolved.

Aum

For I am holy,
and I am sacred
and I am beloved of God.

Aum

Gently and slowly, allow yourself to come out of this posture.

The Mummy Posture

The purpose of the mummy posture is: **to create the state of infinite love of self.**

This posture seals you in your own love. When you cross the right ankle over the left, it blocks outside energy from entering your field and body. And, when you cross your arms over your heart center, the Divine Flow of Love is sealed in. Your female is giving love, tenderness and compassion to your male while He is giving strength, wisdom, power and protection to Her. In this posture, you feel relaxed and complete. You have come into balance with your male and female.

In the mummy, you will be holding yourself in your own love and light, finding peace, fulfillment and contentment within yourself. There is a meridian at the top of the arms where you place your hands, which allows love to enter your heart chakra from the male and female or positive and negative energy flows. This creates total balance within. The energy is moving in a figure 8, the symbol of infinity. Infinite love of self is felt energetically, which leads to accepting the male, or doer in us. It also leads to letting go of expectations of self and our feelings of failure. The female begins to appreciate all that the male is doing in life to provide for her. And the male, in turn, dedicates His life to loving, protecting and providing for the female. She, then can be the love that nourishes him.

Place the right ankle over the left. Cross your arms over the heart center forming an X over your heart. The right arm is over the left. Now, place the left hand on the upper right arm just below the shoulder. Then, place the right hand on the upper left arm just below the shoulder. (Fig. 34)

(Fig. 34)

PRAYER

I protect myself,
for I am safe within myself:
safe to dwell within my
own Love of Self
and Love of God.

Aum

Rest in this posture for a few moments until you feel complete. Then, slowly and gently release your hands and feet, roll to your side coming into the fetal position. Then, use your hands to assist you to come into a seated position.

Chapter 22

The Principle of Desire and Will

We each have an inner female and inner male within us even though we are expressing through either a male or female embodiment. The purpose of the desire and will posture and prayer is to bring harmony and balance within our own male and female. The divinity of the third chakra, which is the Goddess—God is developed as you practice the posture and prayers. The aspect of the Goddess that you will be developing is her desire. **The Goddess is the energy of desire. Her function is to desire to serve God, to feel her love for the God within (her male counterpart) and the God In All That Is.** She does this through **yielding to her male counterpart, desiring to love him.** And he, in turn, **desires to serve her. He serves her through honoring her desires, which are her feelings and intuition and through his deeds and actions. He also serves the Goddess within himself and the Goddess In All That Is in the same way.**

In working with this posture, you will find that it **is no longer your human will, but divine will, that will lead you home into God's Kingdom.**

The energy that turns the key in this posture is desire. **You must feel the essence and energy of pure desire. Desire is without need or desperation. It is not commanding or controlling.** Through the process of feeling desire, you become the pure essence of the Goddess and her energy of desire.

In order to bring balance and harmony within, both the female and male must fulfill their functions. The function of the female is to lead the male home to God, desiring to serve God. The function of the male is to serve the female and to honor her feelings. The will fulfills the desires of the Goddess. **The Goddess and her desire is the spark behind the flame. The flame is the will of God. She must be filled with a burning desire to ignite the flame. The stronger the desire, the greater the flame.** Jesus says: ***The flesh is to be illuminated by the light that is ignited within (female function), and birthed forth into life (male function). The male gives birth to the light through his actions and deeds.***

As the third chakra is developed, the breath of manifestation will occur spontaneously. The energy of desire will be released from within the third chakra and it will move up the chakra system and out the top of your head. The muscles in the third chakra will contract, pumping the energy, while the breath spontaneously assists and moves the energy up and out. As this phenomena occurs, **you are literally becoming the true essence of desire and will.**

Teaching from Jesus, ***Your desire and will must be in harmony, both in service to the unfoldment of the Christ in you.*** This means that the Goddess in you must have a pure desire to know God, to serve God, to feel God and to be one with God. The will must be ready to serve the Goddess through his actions and deeds, honoring the Goddess and her desires.

In life, men that have a powerful woman behind them go forth to accomplish miracles, bringing bountiful fruit home to the Goddess. The female is to believe in and have faith in her male within and in the man in her life. Women, if you find doubt or weakness in your mate, this is the same weakness that is within your inner male. If you are judging or criticizing your mate, you are judging and condemning your own male within. If you love him in his weakness, encourage, praise and believe in him, he will grow to fulfill his destiny. The male is to serve the female, honoring and caring about her feelings and intuition. When the male is in service to the female, he is living according to his divine nature and he is fulfilled. He truly wants to provide abundantly for her, protect her, care for her and satisfy her sexually. He needs the love, approval and encouragement of the female in order to serve her fully.

Honor is a quality of the knight. As the male grows and feels less threatened, he is able to honor the female because he is empowered by her. Men, if you are not honoring the feelings and intuition of the female in your life, you are not honoring the feminine within you. A man who honors his female within and the woman in his life, honors himself.

Honor is born when you live your heart's desire. This is creating dominion over your life. In the state of honor, there is no settling for less than what your heart desires.

Jesus gave me this teaching in October 1998. *Your prayers must be pure and honest in coming from the heart of your hearts, coming from the sweetness of your soul.* **They must be filled with desire and they will be fulfilled. The moment you desire with a pure heart is when you will receive.** *Dive deep into your soul, bringing your desires to the God within, the source of all of your good. Once you send forth your desire, let God (the male) bring it to you. The how, the when, the where is left to God. It will come into form even greater than you could have imagined. Trust God to bring to you your desires and let God do his work. Do not engage your ego mind. If fears and doubts begin to plague you, surrender them. Return to accepting and trusting the power of God (your male).*

As we become desire and choose to serve God, the will of God springs forth from our soul and fulfills our desires (manifestation). This principle, when realized in relationships, creates harmony,

joy, and an abundant shared life. Each is then fulfilling her/his function and purpose. The power struggle is then over in relationships between men and women.

Teaching from Jesus, *Putting God first—this is the right way to live, and assures that your life will be fruitful and bountiful. All your needs will be provided for abundantly.*

As you become desire, the old energy of control and dominance will be dissolved and you will be free to create from within yourself peace and harmony between your own male and female self. This will be mirrored in your male–female relationships in this human dimension.

DESIRE AND WILL EXERCISES

As children, many of us were criticized. No one believed in us or encouraged us so our male energy became damaged. The female also became damaged if we were rejected for a part of our intuition, our love, joy or innocence. As damaged and wounded ones, we didn't grow in godliness.

Now, take a look at how **desire and will** have been working in your life by asking the child within (the wounded self) these questions.

Are you ready to feel your desire to know God? Write what you find.

Is it your will to serve God? Write what you find.

_____

_____

_____

If you found resistance in your child, go back to the first instance where you were wounded and begin to help her/him to correct the error in consciousness. Begin to whisper the truth of God to her/him. Continue to work with the child until she/he is ready to accept the truth.

Take a moment and look at **willingness** in your life by reflecting on these questions.

Are you willing to honor your feelings? This is honoring your feminine.

_____

How? _____

_____

The Goddess is the intuitive part of your. Are you willing to honor your desires and your intuition?

How? _____

_____

In you relationship with your partner, do you choose to serve him/her?

_____

Are you willing to honor his/her feelings and intuition?

If you found resistance, find out why. Write down what you are resisting.

_____

_____

_____

_____

Now that you have found your belief or distorted perception, you can begin to correct it by whispering the truth to yourself. Jesus often whispered the truth to me in my morning meditations. For a half an hour or more, he would repeat one single truth over and over until I began to accept it and let it in. As I let the truth in, I usually cried as my wall of fear and the old belief was dissolving. Now, I whisper and repeat over and over to myself whatever truth I need to embody so that I can change my consciousness and become that truth. This may take a day, a week, a month or longer, depending on how large the blockage or how deep the wound is that we are in the process of healing. Here is an example of whispering the truth to yourself. If you found a belief that you can't trust your intuition: you would whisper to yourself: You can trust your intuition. There's something within you that knows. You repeat it over and over until you begin to feel it inside. Jesus says that we have specific cells that make up the subconscious mind. As children, whatever we were told or perceived as true is what was recorded in the subconscious mind. We can reprogram the subconscious mind by repeating the truth over and over each day until the old programing is completely dissolved and a new program is in place.

The Desire And Will Posture

POSTURE FOR THE LEFT SIDE

Begin with the right leg straight out in front of you. Bend the left knee and bring the left leg over the right, planting the left foot on the mat just outside of the right knee. (The female crosses over the male.)

Bring the right arm around the left knee, pulling the knee toward your chest. Sit up straight and tall, lifting up out of the rib cage and elongating your spine. Raise your left arm, gazing at your left hand as you slowly bring this hand behind you twisting your torso and shoulders. When you can go no further, bring your left hand down to the mat and place it as close to the buttocks as possible. (Fig.35)

As you breathe in, lift up out of your rib cage elongating your spine, and as you breathe out, twist your torso to the left, keeping your buttocks on the mat. Repeat this several more times by breathing in and elongating the spine, then breathing out and twisting.

The Breath of Manifestation may spontaneously occur. You may begin to breathe very rapidly as the energy of **desire** is released from the third chakra. This energy will move up and out the top of your head, cascading all around you.

If you are ready to come into harmony with your male-female within, then say the prayers, feeling the words as they spring forth from deep within your gut (solar plexus).

(Fig.35)

PRAYER

Desire I am. Desire I am.
Desire I am.
I desire to live for you
my Beloved God.
I desire to know you fully
and to serve you fully.

Aum

POSTURE FOR THE RIGHT SIDE

Begin with the left leg straight out in front of you. Bend the right knee and bring the right leg over the left, planting the right foot on the mat just outside of the left knee. (The male crosses over the female.)

Bring the left arm around the right knee, pulling the knee toward your chest. Sit up straight and tall, lifting up out of the rib cage and elongating your spine. Raise your right arm, gazing at your right hand as you slowly bring this hand behind you twisting your torso and shoulders. When you can go no further, bring your right hand down to the mat and place it as close to the buttocks as possible. (Fig. 36)

As you breathe in, lift up out of your rib cage elongating your spine, and as you breath out, twist your torso to the right, keeping your buttocks on the mat. Repeat this several more times by breathing in and elongating the spine, then breathing out and twisting.

The Breath of Manifestation may spontaneously occur. You may begin to breathe very rapidly as the energy of **will** is released from the third chakra. This energy will move up and out the top of your head cascading all about you.

If you are ready to begin to come into harmony with your feelings and knowingness, then say the prayer from deep within you.

(Fig. 36)

PRAYER

I will to honor you
my Goddess.
I will to serve you.
I will to serve God.

Aum

Chapter 23

Bringing God Into Visible Form
Through Gratitude & Faith

A teaching from Jesus: *By loving and worshipping God, you accomplish all that is needed. By blessing and thanking God, you bring God into visible form in your life. This is the path to attain all of God's wisdom and knowledge. Man must bring the body and soul into one force to bring the Holy Spirit through him.*

By loving and worshipping God, you feel the beauty of God and the oneness with God. What else is needed? This love and oneness is all we ever have wanted, what we have searched for. In this state of being, we feel incredible oneness and we bless all of our problems which dissolves them. They are no longer consuming us with worry, doubt and fear. Then, our minds are clear, open to receive divine wisdom and inspiration from the Mind of God. Our bodies are light and we feel pleasure moving through them.

I have found that I am clear enough in this state of oneness that I can see my illusions and I realize that everything is in divine order. I can bless God for my challenges, seeing that they have been what caused me to expand into this wonder of God. Yes, my so called problems have been my greatest blessings because they helped me accomplish what was needed for me to move to the next level spiritually.

When I thank God for my good, I am believing in God's love for me. My heart is open to give love to God and to receive blessings from God. When my ego mind is saying, *where will my good come from*, it cannot conceive of the miracle because it is outside the Kingdom, trapped in its limited thinking. By thanking God for my good, I suddenly move beyond my limitation and the fear is gone and I can trust God's will to bring into form my good. Then my ego mind isn't saying, *how will it come, where is it coming from and when will it come.* I am trusting that God's plan is perfect and I don't need to know how, where and when. This, for me is freedom. Joy is in my heart and excitement fills my spirit as I wait to see the miracle come into form. It is just like waiting to open my Christmas presents that are wrapped perfectly. **As you thank God for loving you, love increases in your life experiences as if love just multiplied. If you want to increase any good in your life, thank God for the good and it will multiply**. Jesus calls this THE LAW OF MULTIPLICATION.

THE PATH TO ATTAIN ALL OF GOD'S WISDOM AND KNOWLEDGE

By loving, worshipping, blessing and thanking God, you become God. This practice of loving, worshipping, blessing and thanking God dissolves the ego mind which is the lack of self love, self worth, guilt, regret, remorse, pain and fear. These limited feelings and thoughts create our separation from God. As we become one, we become as God is: love, grace, goodness, wisdom, knowledge, power (all that we really are). Remember, we have been told we already know everything and you will experience knowing through loving, worshipping, blessing and thanking God.

Bringing The Holy Spirit Through You

As we practice loving, worshipping, blessing and thanking God, our soul is purified and our body begins to hold a higher and higher vibrational rate. The body begins to clear cellularly. Then the body and soul become one force which allows the Holy Spirit to move freely through the body. The ego is being tamed of its needs for physical, emotional and mental gratification. The needs and addictions of the body will dissipate because the feelings and experiences of beauty, love, and pleasure that come from bringing the Holy Spirit through you feel so much more gratifying than the needs of the body.

It takes practice to change the way you relate to the force of good (known as God) in the universe. As you are thanking God for your good, you are accepting good to flow to you. Good is all around you. Thanking God for your good, draws it to you.

I invite you to become still and focus within and then repeat this prayer of thanksgiving until you feel the quickening in your soul. Choose an area for which you are thankful and fill in the blank.

*I thank you, beloved God for*_____
*I thank you, beloved God for*_____
*I thank you, beloved God for*_____

Even though you may not feel the quickening within yourself, I encourage you to continue the practice and one day you will have the experience of bringing God into visible form through thankfulness.

Jesus gave me this wisdom on thankfulness in October 1998. **Thank God for the blessings He bestows upon you. Stay in the state of thankfulness. Do not repeat your request. Stay focused in the state of thankfulness expecting God's good to be delivered to you**. This is the path to attain wisdom and knowledge. This, then leads to the Law of Faith.

FAITH

A teaching from Jesus: *When you are thanking God for your good, the desire is implanted into your soul and the vibration of the soul* *is quickened through the Law of Faith. God is love, and when you have faith, it allows God to dissolve your fears and bring into form your desired result. You must believe that the Father within will bring you what you have asked for. Thank Him for bringing this gift to you. When you have faith, you are trusting yourself and the Father within.*

As you move into your own Christ Consciousness, surrendering the old ways of being, have faith that the Father within shall bring you into the Kingdom of Heaven—into the true joy and abundance of life.

You must have faith and KNOW ALL THINGS ARE POSSIBLE WITH GOD. If you live the life of truth and love knowing and believing, nothing will be denied you and all will be possible. If you believe that you can become a Christ and have faith doing the work of the Father, you shall do greater works than I.

The secret of life is getting at-one-ment in consciousness and holding firmly and purely to the truth. FAITH, FAITH, FAITH, no doubt, no fear. Blessings to you and walk in faith.

I invite you to develop your faith and live in the state of expectancy. Expect good to be in your life by thanking God for it even before it arrives. Faith is what allows you to heal. Faith is what brings your dreams into form. Faith is the state of allowing. Allowing God to love you is a form of self-love. When we love ourselves, we let ourselves have what we want. **Then, your heart is open to receive.**

FAITH IS FOUND IN THE HEART CHAKRA

Jesus says: *Each must display his own faith to enter the Kingdom of God's wealth.*

MY EXPERIENCE OF THANKSGIVING & FAITH
(Faith Becomes Knowing Through Experience)

In the summer of 1997, I was asked to cancel all of my traveling events during the month of July so that I would be able to stay home and write my yoga book. I live in Palm Desert, California, where the temperatures raise to 120 degrees in the summer. A large portion of the population leave after spending the winter months in this desert paradise.

It was the perfect time to stay in and write, as the heat of the day kept me homebound in the comfort of air conditioning. However, I had one big problem since my usual clients for healings were gone for the summer and my yoga classes were over for the season. **How was I to support myself financially?** I soon became very fearful and remember going to my health club to take a steam. Alone in the steam room and crying aloud, I told Jesus how scared I was. He replied that he would provide for me because I was doing the Fathers work. With this news, I cried even harder in relief and thankfulness. **I believed him and had faith that I would be provided for. I began thanking God over and over again for bringing me the money to live.**

Soon after I returned home, the phone rang with a request for healing from the husband of a friend. **Again, I felt such gratitude that I started to thank and bless God.** While still in prayer, the phone rang again. This time a woman wanted a series of four healings. **I was overjoyed and overwhelmed by the results of my prayers and God's goodness.** The month continued and I kept thanking God for bringing me the money I needed. Most of the day and into the night, I was in total joy writing. The money kept coming and it turned out to be one of my most prosperous months of 1997 for me. I completed the yoga portion of the book and I was so very happy and fulfilled. Through the process of thanksgiving and faith, I had released a tremendous amount of survival fear.

The experience of your prayers being answered will bring you joy. Your faith and your power will grow. As this occurs for you, your prayers will be answered more rapidly. Soon, your miracles will become larger and more magnificent as you move into the state of knowing. In the state of knowing, there is no fear or doubt.

KNOWING IS FOUND IN THE SEVENTH SACRED SEAL

Gratitude And Faith Postures

You have already accepted the truth that you are always loved. Now, you are expressing your gratitude to God for loving you. From a seated position, bend your right knee, crossing it over the left bent knee. Sit back between your heels. If possible, keep your right knee aligned directly over your left. Place your hands on your feet, hinge from the hips and bring your head as close to your knees as you can. (Fig. 37)

Feel the beauty of your body as you speak the prayer of gratitude. **Feel the energy moving in your body as it comes into perfect balance, harmony and health.**

(Fig. 37)

PRAYER

Thank you Beloved Father for healing me.
Thank you for bringing my glands into perfect harmony and balance.
Thank you for my perfect health.
Thank you! Thank you!

Aum

From a seated position, bend your left knee, crossing it over the right bent knee. Sit back between your heels. If possible, keep your left knee aligned directly over your right. Place your hands on your feet, hinge from the hips and bring your head as close to your knees as you can. (Fig. 38)

Feel your gratitude as you pray aloud. **Feel your love and the love that is enveloping you as you speak the words, acknowledging the love that is loving you right now.**

(Fig. 38)

PRAYER

I thank you my Beloved God
for loving me. I thank you for holding me
in the arms of love.
I thank you for filling my life with love.

Aum

Heart-felt Gratitude

This series of movements (Fig. 39, 40 & 41) are symbolic and hold the energy of joy. They create within you the Essene Cross as they open the pathways for the energy to flow both vertically and horizontally in the symbol of the cross. Jesus says that the Essene Cross is the symbol of joy. When you are in the state of gratitude, you are in the state of joy.

Bringing your hands together in a prayer position in front of the heart center joins the two polarities of female and male or negative and positive energy. This instantly begins to bring inner balance to you.

Your knees are directly connected to the heart chakra or center. As you are kneeling, your heart chakra will begin to expand. You have heard the saying.. As above, so below. This is true in the body. There are hinges within the knee chakras that open your heart. That is why for eons, people have dropped to their knees instinctively in prayer and reverence. When a man proposes marriage to his maiden, he drops to his knees and bears his heart and love to her, asking for her love in return. Many people also get on their knees when asking for forgiveness because they are speaking from their heart centers.

The movements that follow (Fig. 39, 40 & 41) are intended to take you into a deep space of heart-filled gratitude which leads you into joy.

Kneel on both knees, placing your hands together in front of your heart chakra in a prayer position. Close your eyes and let your heart open. Begin to thank God for your heart's desire. (Fig. 39)

(Fig. 39)

PRAYER

Thank you Beloved Father for my life.
Thank your for filling my life with abundance.

Aum

Feel the pleasure of living in your heart center, experiencing reigning in your kingdom.

When you are in the state of gratitude, you may find that your heart begins to open even more as you lean back. (Fig. 40)

(Fig. 40)

Once the energy has moved out through your crown chakra, bow down in reverence. Bend at the hips, bringing your forehead down and rest it on the floor as your arms extend out in front of your head. Place your hands palms down on the floor. (Fig. 41)

(Fig. 41)

Begin to rest in the energy of gratitude.

Chapter 24

The Principle of Being

This principle is: **Being available for God to love you and fill your world with the abundance of God's wealth.** This state of being is you, purely you without needs or attachments to outcomes. **You are in the present moment being loved by the God within.** There is no worry or doubt. You have surrendered the fear and you are trusting that God is caring for you. **This is a receptive state where you have yielded to being consumed with love.**

In the state of being, there is nothing that we have to do. In our culture, we have been trained to perform and compete since childhood. We are praised for how we look, how athletic we are, how smart we are and how polite and good we behave. The ego gets into the pattern of wanting and needing more of everything: praise, money, cars; everything in the material world. So we are caught up in having to be a success, living a certain life-style, holding a certain job and driving a specific kind of car. It is a consciousness where we work and achieve to have all the material things, all the right friends and belong to all the appropriate clubs to bring us status. **This sets up a behavior pattern of doing to receive love.** We begin to believe that we are loved for what we have, what we do or how we look. We build a false perception of ourselves, of love and of life.

We have forgotten that what is important is our state of being. Even though we may have all the success and the relationships that say we are loved and wanted, inside, there is great emptiness. **We are not yet filled with God's love.** Our ego still has needs to have more: whether it is love, power, money, sex, success. **We will never be satisfied until we are being love.**

In truth, it is not what you are doing that is important, but, how you are being doing it. It does not matter what the task is or how mundane it may be. How are you being while doing the task? Are you happy, relaxed, peaceful, fulfilled?

THE TRUTH IS THAT YOU ARE LOVE
YOU ARE GOD IN HUMAN FORM
YOU ARE THE INDIVIDUAL ESSENCE OF YOUR SPIRIT

In the state of being, you have dissolved the false concepts of self, of love and of life. This frees you to begin to feel the God you are loving you. God's blissful energy moves up the spine into the entire body. You are consumed with your own love, loving you. This love penetrates every cell in your body.

My experience of this is hard to put into words. The ecstasy of this pleasure is delicious. This energy takes me into higher and higher states of bliss, consuming me and bringing me into a state of love that is not of this world. I feel God loving me from the inside out with every cell receiving this energy of love. In these moments of oneness, I feel safe, loved and cared for. **I need nothing from outside of me. I have everything I could ever want inside of me. I can be me without the need to get anything or the need to be anything but what I am in the moment. There is nothing to prove to myself or anyone. I can trust God even more with my life, feeling that God is there loving me, filling every need I might have.**

This is a relaxed state of **fulfillment**. You begin to let the love of God dissolve the areas of stress, pain and tension that you have held in your body. You will experience this as pleasure. **This pleasure of being loved is so fulfilling and overflowing that love will be expressed from you through your eyes, your smile and your touch.** Love will be in your energy field and it will draw more love from the world around. **You will exist in a river of love.** God will deliver good to you without any effort on your part.

THE FATHER AND I ARE ONE
and THE FATHER BRINGS ME ALL THINGS
are the realizations in your being.

Being Postures

Sit straight and tall, extending your right leg out in front of you. Bend your left knee and place your left foot in toward the inner right thigh. Keep your back straight, begin to hinge forward from the hips (Fig. 42) in blessing and thanksgiving. Let the Grace of God move you forward.

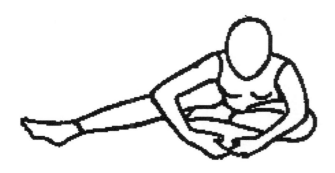

(Fig. 42)

PRAYER

I yield to you Beloved God of my Being.
I no longer need to do anything to be loved.
I no longer need to prove anything to myself or anyone else.
I am perfect as I am.
I am loved as I am.

Aum

Let the energy move your body back to a seated position. Close your eyes and feel the energy within and around you. **Let the energy have full sway in your body as you yield to God's love for you**. Again, allow the energy to move through you.

Sit straight and tall, extending your left leg out in front of you. Bend your right knee and place your right foot in toward the inner left thigh. Keep your back straight, begin to hinge forward from the hips (Fig. 43) in blessing and thanksgiving. Let the Grace of God move you forward.

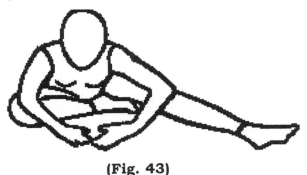

(Fig. 43)

PRAYER

You are all that I want.
You are all that I need.
I am yours. I trust you with my life.
Consume me with your love
Beloved Mother-Father God.

Feel the pleasure of God's love for you as you allow this love to embrace you. Again, allow the energy to move through your body.

I am being loved.
I am being held in the arms of love.
Thank you Beloved Mother-Father God.
Aum

The Angel Of Mastery

Chapter 25

Holy Communion

Jesus teaches us to : ***Accept your Divine Spirit. Hold Holy Communion each day with this Divine source of wisdom and love for you. In this way, you become your divine essence.***

Begin to realize that you are one with God, that the divine essence of God is within you and around you, always loving you and waiting to support you, waiting to bring you whatever you might need. The truth is waiting to set you free. **When we hold Holy Communion with the divine essence of God, we are given the truth to take us out of the illusion that we have been experiencing and dwelling in**. As we accept the truth, we rapidly begin to move into another vibration, another reality.

We create our lives from the vibrations we are transmitting to the universe. We magnetize to us a like frequency to match what we are transmitting. As we continue to accept the truth, we are raising our vibrations and a new life is then created as we magnetize new experiences of living in love, joy, freedom and abundance. This is all done effortlessly, for we are a new being with new truths. We live a life that is in alignment to God's Will for us. We are becoming as God is: goodness, grace, love, wisdom and power.

Stand in conscious communion with God and the confusion of the world cannot touch you. The world around you may be experiencing confusion, disaster, even chaos. As you practice daily communion with God, you will be brought the truth of why this is occurring and your divine purpose or the action you need to take. Clearly, you can see that everything is in divine order moving toward peace and love. You remain in a state of tranquillity as you move through what others may judge or view as chaos. The circumstances of life no longer own you. Therefore, you can walk through the confusion in a state of certainty, joy and even excitement knowing something wonderful is waiting for you. As you accept and embrace the truth God brings you in Holy Communion, you will experience a new life, being reborn over and over a million times.

In the state of Holy Communion, we are developing the Seventh Sacred Seal. Jesus says that within the human brain there are cells that are specifially designed to communicate with the Divine Mind of God. As you continue to use the prayers in Shakti Yoga, you will activate these divine cells to be able to receive wisdom from the Noble Mind of God. We all have the ability to know all that we need to know in any given moment.

The Chakras In Holy Communion

All seven chakras begin a sacred movement in this practice of Holy Communion. Jesus calls this movement, the **creation of heaven and earth within you**. Within each chakra is a pyramid shaped symbol. In the lower three chakras, the pyramid is facing downward. In the upper three chakras, the pyramid is facing upward. In the heart center, there are two pyramids, one facing downward and one facing upward. (Fig. 44)

(Fig. 44)

The purpose of Holy Communion is to create union between heaven and earth within you. As we move into the state of Holy Communion, our purpose is to flip the pyramids so that the lower pyramids are facing upward **releasing life force into the body**, and the upper pyramids flip downward bringing the divine flow into the body. Simultaneously, these two energies meet in the heart causing the two pyramids in the heart chakra to flip **forming the Star of David**. (Fig. 45)

In the moment that the energy of your Divine Essence and your Life Force join in the heart, the Star of David begins to spin creating a combustion of energy which leaves your heart center in a spiral.

My experience of this holy moment was beyond anything I had ever known. I was by myself doing my Yoga in Hawaii. Suddenly, the energy began to ascend which was usual for me. In the past, the energy went all the way up and out of the crown chakra. On this day, the energy also began to move downward toward my heart. **The two energies met and the light was a burst of power in my heart chakra, spinning round and round, leaving my body as a combustion of light with a force that was new to me.**

As soon as this occurred, I was told that a **holy matrimony had taken place within my physical body joining my Human Self with my Divine Self creating the union of heaven and earth within me**. A great sense of oneness and peace has been with me ever since. I am no longer separate from my divinity and I have access to information and wisdom that was not possible before.

(Fig. 45)

Every time we think that something or someone outside of us is the source of our good, our happiness, or our financial abundance; we are leaking our life force. The body becomes weakened, our emotions become unbalanced and many times we feel emptiness, or a sense of lack, or a sense of loss and loneliness, or even a sense of being unloved. Every time we feel out of control or powerless because we have allowed someone else to take our power away through force, manipulation or the fear of losing their approval; we are depleting ourselves of joy, power and life force energy. We begin to feel helpless, hopeless, submissive, powerless and even desperate. When we are in those feelings, the pyramids face downward and the energy is leaving our lower chakras. We are literally bleeding away our life force.

When we look at anyone (an attractive person) or anything (new car) and lust after them, wanting to possess them, we again leak our life force energy. The energy is leaving our body and going directly to the person or thing. **Having or desiring wonderful people or things in our lives is not the error here. It is when we lust for someone or thing outside of us because we don't feel that who we are and what we are is enough that we hold an error in our consciousness. We think that we need someone or something to be whole.**

When we engage in these forms of third dimensional reality, **the energy from our lower chakras leaves our body and goes to the person or object through attraction. The person or object now has a part of us and an energetic cord is established between that person or object and us**. If the energetic cord is with another person, we often find ourselves angry at them for controlling us or not loving us. Sometimes we spend years dissolving this energy cord.

CONSERVING YOUR LIFE FORCE

As we evolve and heal, we enter a state where we are conserving our life force. We are looking within ourselves for our good and our lower chakras are feeding us life force, rejuvenating our bodies. This is because we are loving ourselves, respecting ourselves and liking who we are.

The myth that we need to be celibate to conserve our life force is not necessarily true. We can enjoy a physical relationship when we realize that our partner is not the Source. Then, we can experience trantra with a partner allowing the life force within the bodies to ascend through the chakras and out the top of the crown.

Wisdom from Jesus on Conserving your Life Force

When you become set in lower consciousness and continue to look outside of yourself for nourishment, for love, for pleasure; then, you begin to age and die. The lower vibrations of your limited thoughts become set, and the new cells are thrown off instead of the old. The old cells then begin to decay and decompose and you age. ***If you continue to receive the truth of God and embrace this truth, you will then be conserving your life force and you will live a long, healthy life, because the old cells are replaced by the new cells and their vibrations of life and truth.***

The key to our development is to learn to allow the life force to come up into the body to regenerate and rejuvenate us. This is obtained by accepting all of our human self, our feelings, our thoughts and our shortcomings without judgment. Accepting our divinity as part of us in every moment is equally important. Accepting that we are not alone, that the Mother-Father (God) is around us always, supporting and loving us, that the Mother-Father (God) is within us and is us. Close your eyes and say this prayer until you feel the Mother-Father within and around you. In this way you will experience this truth within.

The Mother–Father God is within me
and I am within the Mother-Father God.

As we accept ourselves with our shortcomings, **we are no longer deny-ing ourselves life**. This opens the flow of life force energy within us, which begins to awaken the body to new life. **When we deny our feelings, we are literally dying.**

As we accept our humanity with all of its unconsciousness, we move into a state of wholeness. **We cannot be holy until we are whole,** until we are receptive to ourselves exactly as we are with love. Remember, the Mother-Father God is here to support all of life and we must open the gateways within us to allow ourselves to receive the wisdom of the Father and the love of the Mother to manifest in our lives.

You will find oneness, wisdom, knowledge and clear guidance in Holy Communion. A deep felt connection to the Source will be experienced. There will be a sense of stillness, of peace. As I lead my classes into this state, Jesus always says to me, *Peace be still.* You may hear direct communication on how to proceed with your life from this Source. You may feel consumed by the grace of God. Some feel the Kundalini energy rising up the spine. If you are one that has inner vision, you will see the beauty of God's life.

Jesus says, *Calm, knowing and power come from oneness with the Father (God) within. Oneness is the greatest power, the greatest security.*

After completing the Shakti Yoga and entering the final phase of Holy Communion, you will be very clear and in a state of oneness with the God within you and around you, which is sustaining all of life. You are now available to receive the wisdom that is needed in your life. You begin to have your own conversation with God, asking for clarity on any issue of concern.

You will want to stay in this state forever. Do stay a while, **for the body must be at peace to heal**. You will be healing very deeply in body, mind and emotions, as your spirit becomes more alive in your body. **This is developing your light body. You are becoming the light of God.**

The Holy Communion Series of Postures

There are three phases in this series of postures and prayers.

THE FIRST PHASE

In the first phase of this posture, we bow to our humanity. Sit in a half lotus or an Indian style position. Place your hands on your knees with your palms facing up. Touch the thumb and the middle two fingers together. This connects the flow of energy known as the Kundalini. Close your eyes and focus on the energy along both sides of the spine. Let your body sway as the energy begins to ascend up the spine. When you touch your thumb (which is neutral) to the inner two fingers (one is positive and the other is negative), you are plugging yourself in to the natural flow of your own female-male or yin-yang energy. Now, sit with your back as erect as possible. (Fig.46)

(Fig.46)

Hinge forward from the hips with a flat back, keeping your sit bones on the mat. Go forward as far a possible without rounding your back. (Fig. 47)

(Fig. 47)

PRAYER

I bow to my human self.
I bow to my fearful self.
I bow to my unworthy self.
I thank you for your courage to feel your pain.
I thank you for the courage to move
through the darkness into the light.
I thank you for trusting me and the God within.
I love you and I need you to walk
with me into the light.
I cannot go forward without you.
We are one now and forever.

Aum

Let the energy move your body upward into a sitting position. **Feel the flow of your life force as it begins its movement up into your body.**

Feel reverence and gratitude for your human self as you prepare to bow.

THE SECOND PHASE

In the second phase of this posture, we bow to our Divinity. The posture is identical to the one used in the first phase.

Once again, sit erect. Continue to have your thumb and the middle two fingers touch. (Fig. 46) Hinge forward from the hips with a flat back.

PRAYER

I bow to my Divine Essence.
I thank You for Your endless
love and patience with me.
I am devoted to You, My Beloved God.
I am devoted to bringing You
forth through my human form.
I give you my life.
I am Yours now and forever.
And so it is.

Aum

Let the energy move your body, returning you to a seated position. **Feel the pleasure of your own Divinity loving you and blessing you as you enter the state of bliss.**

THE THIRD PHASE

The third phase of this posture is an active meditation. It is an acknowledgment of the female and male aspects of Divinity within us, as well as, a time of direct communication with the Divine Mind of God.

ACTIVE MEDITATION FOR THE FEMININE LIGHT

Bring your attention and awareness down to the base of your spine on the left side. Focus on the feminine energy on the left side of the spine. You may see this as a beautiful pink light. With your thoughts, begin to bring the feminine energy up your spine, guiding it to the solar plexus and then to the heart center as you breathe into your heart. Direct the energy up to your throat and all the way out the top of your head. This creates a fountainhead for the pink light to cascade all around you. **Feel the bliss of your feminine light soothing you and loving you.**

PRAYER OF ACKNOWLEDGMENT

I am my Feminine Light.
I am the Goddess of Creation.
I am the Divine Mother.
I am the Goddess.
I am the Queen.
I am the Priestess.
I am the Purity of the Maiden.

Aum

ACTIVE MEDITATION FOR THE MASCULINE LIGHT

Bring your attention and awareness to the right side of your spine. You may see this as a beautiful blue light. Focus on directing the male energy up your spine to the third chakra, your solar plexus. Feel the blue light moving up into your heart, filling your heart center. Direct your male energy to the throat and then all the way out the top of your head, feeling the energy as it cascades all around you. **Feel the strength and power of your male energy as it anoints you.**

PRAYER OF ACKNOWLEDGMENT

I am the Passion to live life fully.
I am the Father within me.
I am the Will of God.
I am the King in My Kingdom.
I am the Priest.
I am the Knight.
And so it is.

Aum

As you complete this meditation. you have created what Jesus calls, *The Fountainhead.* Both the pink, feminine light and the blue, male light and energy are coming out of the crown and cascading all around the body. You are bathed in your own love and light. (Fig. 48)

(Fig. 48)The Fountainhead

HOLY COMMUNION

Communication directly to GOD,
THE INFINITE MIND

Now that our crown chakra is open, we enter the Kingdom of Light, where all is available and waiting for us. All of the answers to every situation, every problem or challenge that we may have, is already existing in THE MIND OF GOD.

PRAYER

Beloved Father-Mother God.
What do I need to see that I cannot see?
What do I need to know?

Let the answer be brought to you. **Be open to receiving Divine impulses of energy from God. Stay in the state of communion as long as you desire.**

Thank you for joining me in this sacred moment of truth. Thank you for joining me in this blessed experience of Shakti Yoga. I love you and thank you for the Divine Essence you bring to life.

Peace be with you and Namaste.

Ongoing Programs Available

I have been blessed with the information found in this book. It has transformed me beyond anything that I thought was possible. The wisdom from Jesus is a gift I share with you and anyone who desires to activate the Christ light within them and who desires to become part of the Second Coming of Christ, creating peace on earth.

If you feel drawn to this work, I offer workshops, healings and retreats. I have also created a certification program for those drawn to Shakti Yoga, either for self use or to lead others in the practice. A healing school is available to all who wish to learn the mysteries of healing as Jesus taught them to me. I call this form of healing Shakti Therapy which includes Radiant Energy Healing with the Keys to the Sacred Seals. This has the power to dissolve blockages within the cellular, emotional and energetic structures of the body.

If you want to stay connected to this work and receive newsletters and schedules of events throughout North America, call **(208) 756-6774 or write to Virginia Ellen, PO Box 345, Salmon. ID., USA, 83467-0345.**